BATTLECRUISERS

Steaming at high speed through a North Sea swell in 1917 Fisher's 'Splendid Cats' were indeed a splendid sight. Nearest the camera is *Tiger* with, in line abreast to starboard, *Princess Royal* and *Lion*, flagship of the Battlecruiser Force throughout the First World War. (Author's collection)

Battlecruisers

John Roberts

CAXTON EDITIONS

Acknowledgements

The author's thanks are due to D K Brown RCNC, Ray Burt, Guy Robbins and the staffs of the National Maritime Museum, London and the Public Record Office for their invaluable assistance. My gratitude is also due to my wife Jean for her infinite patience, encouragement and very real help during the preparation of this work.

First published in Great Britain in 1997 by Chatham Publishing, 61 Frith Street, London W1V 5TA

This edition published 2003 by Caxton Editions
an imprint of The Caxton Publishing Group

British Library Cataloguing in Publication Data
A catalogue record for this book is available from the British Library

ISBN 1 84067 530 6

Printed in Dubai

Contents

Abbreviations

AA. Anti-aircraft
ADNC. Assistant Director of Naval Construction (this was not a singular post)
AEW. Admiralty Experiment Works
AP. Armour piercing (shell)
APC. Armour piercing capped (shell)
ATB. Anti torpedo-boat (guns)

BCS. Battlecruiser Squadron
BL. Breech loading

c. circa
cal. calibre
C-in-C. Commander-in-Chief
C and M. Care and Maintenance
CP. Common pointed (shell)
CPC. Common pointed capped (shell)
crh. calibre radius head
CS. Cruiser Squadron
CT. Conning tower

DNC. Director of Naval Construction

DNI. Director of Naval Intelligence
DNO. Director of Naval Ordnance

efc. equivalent full charge
E-in-C. Engineer-in-Chief

fps. feet per second

GCT. Gun control tower

HA. High angle
HE. High explosive
HP. High pressure
HT. High tensile (steel)

ihp. indicated horse power

KC. Krupp Cemented (armour)
KNC. Krupp Non-Cemented (armour)

LCS. Light Cruiser Squadron
LP. Low pressure

LWL. Load water line

MS. Mild Steel

NS. Nickel steel

pdr. pounder (gun)

QF. quick-firing

RMA. Royal Marine Artillery
RMLI. Royal Marine Light Infantry
rpg. rounds per gun
rpm. revolutions per minute

shp. shaft horse power
SW. Steel wire (hawsers)

TS. Transmitting station

TT. Torpedo tube(s)

WO. Warrant Officer
WT. Wireless transmitter

Introduction

Between 1900 and 1914 the Royal Navy underwent a rapid revolutionary change as a result of a combination of major technical developments and the arrival at a senior level of officers who were ready and willing to to use these developments to maintain Britain's position as the world's leading naval power. These changes effectively resulted in the total replacement of the frontline ships of the fleet with vessels that were larger, more powerful and, in what was expected to be the conditions of a modern naval war, more capable. This was, however, undertaken without direct experience of such a war and to a large extent the success or otherwise of the fleet depended on the accuracy of the decisions and assumptions made by these officers. Foremost among their number was Admiral Sir John Fisher, First Sea Lord 1904-11, who initiated what was to become known as the Dreadnought Revolution – the introduction of the fast, all-big-gun battleship, driven by turbine machinery. On the material side this should have been Fisher's greatest achievement but he was inclined to believe that the day of the battleship was over because they were too vulnerable to the torpedo and mine. He saw the future in the development of torpedo craft, particularly the submarine, and the armoured cruiser, but his writings on this subject are confused. The obvious conclusion to draw from Fisher's statements is that he considered that torpedo craft and mines would take care of naval operations in European waters while the armoured cruiser would secure the deep ocean against commerce raiders. He did not, however, make as clear a statement as this and also indicated that the armoured cruiser could replace the battleship in fleet operations, without explaining why such a vessel was not equally at risk from the mine and torpedo. The Royal Navy's attachment to the battleship was, however, too strong for even Fisher to break and he accepted, sometimes with little grace, that the construction of these vessels would have to continue. The armoured cruiser, with the provision of the same all-big-gun armament of the battleship, became the battlecruiser and was integrated with the Dreadnought fleet to serve as a scouting force and as a fast wing for the battle squadrons. However, Fisher continued to maintain that the battlecruiser was the capital ship of the future because he considered its high speed would be the key to success in a naval war.

The construction of the battlecruisers was somewhat patchy, for reasons that will become clear later, and they fall into a number of basic sub-groups. The pre-war ships divide neatly between those armed with 12in guns and those armed with 13.5in guns, the former representing the direct armoured cruiser derivatives while the latter moved closer to the designation of fast battleships. The first group consisted of two classes – the *Invincible* class (*Invincible*, *Inflexible* and *Indomitable*) and the *Indefatigable* class (*Indefatigable*, *Australia* and *New Zealand*). The second group of four ships, *Lion*, *Princess Royal*, *Queen Mary* and *Tiger* were of clearly related design but only the first two were direct sisters. The design of the last two ships of the first group overlapped that of the first ships of the second group and this parallel construction of both the new and old types is one of the peculiarities of the pre-war construction programmes. The battlecruisers constructed during the war show a much more diverse pattern and are actually distinguished entirely by the

The first battlecruiser, *Indomitable*, shortly after completion in 1908. (MoD)

class they belonged to. The first two, *Renown* and *Repulse*, were effectively a repetition of the original battlecruiser concept of 1905, while the next three, the large light cruisers of the *Courageous* type, are so unusual as to defy attempts at classification. The last battlecruiser of this era, *Hood*, moved the entire concept forward into the fast battleship class and, being the only vessel of the type entirely free of Fisher's influence, gives a good indication of the expectations of the other officers involved in the development of the type – in particular Admiral Jellicoe.

The battlecruiser type was the subject of considerable controversy prior to the First World War when many saw them as very expensive vessels which could carry out no obvious function that a more conventional cruiser type could not fulfil. Nevertheless, they caught the public imagination and gained a reputation as the 'glamour' ships of the fleet – a reputation enhanced during the war by their being under the command of the charismatic Rear-Admiral David Beatty – the archetypal naval hero.

The battlecruisers were involved in a number of minor skirmishes during the war but only three major battles. The first of these, the Battle of the Falkland Islands, took place on 8 December 1914 and was remarkable for being an almost perfect example of the type of action originally envisaged by Fisher for his new ships. The main battle was, moreover, fought between two ships of the first group of British battlecruisers, the *Invincible* and *Inflexible*, and two of the most modern of Germany's armoured cruisers, the *Scharnhorst* and *Gneisenau*. Both German ships were sunk with heavy loss of life but this was by no means easily accomplished. The *Scharnhorst* did not sink until three hours after the commencement of action and the *Gneisenau* lasted two hours longer, the British ships expending the majority of their ammunition in the process (*Invincible* 513 and *Inflexible* 661 12in shells). There were reasons for this apparently poor performance in that the British were seriously hampered by their own funnel smoke, the action involved a considerable amount of manoeuvring and the battlecruisers were deliberately kept at long range in the hope of avoiding as much damage as possible by keeping to the extreme range of the German guns. All this worked against the accuracy of the ships' fire control systems and limited the percentage of hits to rounds fired to a very low figure. However, it is worth bearing in mind that in 1904 Fisher was anticipating a marked advantage in long-range fire for British ships and this was in part used as a basis to justify the battlecruiser type.

The battlecruisers' second major battle was the Dogger Bank, fought in the southern North Sea on 24 January 1915 and for the first time this saw them in action against their opposite numbers of the German 1st Scouting Group. The fight consisted entirely of a long stern chase in which the British ships, in the order *Lion* (flagship), *Tiger*, *Princess Royal*, *New Zealand* and *Indomitable* pursued the German ships in the order *Seydlitz* (flagship), *Moltke*, *Derfflinger* and *Blücher* towards the latters' base. The action was largely fought at high speed with the faster British ships gradually overhauling the German squadron which was held back in support of the *Blücher*, a hybrid armoured cruiser which was considerably slower than her companions. Fire was opened at very long range and with both sides hampered by problems of visibility it was some time before any hits were scored by either side. Most damage was suffered by the ships closest to the enemy – the *Blücher* at the stern of the German line and the *Lion* at the head of the British line. The *Blücher* suffered steadily mounting damage as she was engaged by each British ship in turn and eventually began to lose speed and drop astern. The *Lion*, although better able to absorb damage, eventually suffered a hit which required her to stop her port engine and she had to retire from action. Unfortunately, confusion resulting from the flagship's signals as she dropped astern led to a misinterpretation of Beatty's intentions and the remaining British ships turned on, and eventually sank, the unfortunate *Blücher* while the rest of the German squadron escaped at high speed. Apart from the obvious recriminations with regard to the escape of the German squadron, the British were comparatively pleased with their performance, believing that they had caused major damage to the enemy ships. In fact, *Blücher* excepted, they scored only three hits each on *Seydlitz* and *Derfflinger* and of these only one, a shell that put both of *Seydlitz*'s after turrets out of action, was serious. In contrast six hits were made on *Tiger* and no less than seventeen on *Lion*. Several lessons that could have been learnt from this battle appear to have received scant attention, particularly the quality of German gunnery and the dangers from long-range fire in which shells fell at steep angles of descent. Both Captain Chatfield of the *Lion* and Rear-Admiral Moore (second-in-command of the Battle-

The German armoured cruiser *Blücher*, the only uniform main armament ship of the type and the obvious logical development for heavy cruisers, was totally outclassed by the battlecruiser. (Author's collection)

Tiger following *Lion*, with *Princess Royal* in the distance, 1917. (Author's collection)

cruiser Force with his flag in *New Zealand*) commented on the dangers posed by the latter and Moore recommended the thickening of protection to turret roofs but their words went unheeded.

The last and most important of the battlecruiser actions was the Battle of Jutland, fought in the eastern part of the North Sea during 31 May-1 June 1916. The battle opened with the meeting of the opposing battlecruiser squadrons, both scouting ahead of their main fleets. The opening moves followed the pattern of the Dogger Bank except that in this case the German Admiral, Hipper, was attempting to draw Beatty south into the arms of the German battlefleet rather than trying to escape. The British ships consisted of *Lion* (flag), *Princess Royal*, *Queen Mary*, *Tiger*, *New Zealand* and *Indefatigable*. They were supported by four of the fast battleships of the 5th Battle Squadron which had been temporarily attached to the Battlecruiser Fleet while Admiral Hood's 3rd Battlecruiser Squadron (*Invincible* [flag], *Indomitable* and *Inflexible*) went north to Scapa Flow for gunnery practice. However, due to a signals failure the battleships took some time to get into action and initially the opposing battlecruisers had only each other to contend with. The German force consisted of *Lützow*, *Derfflinger*, *Seydlitz*, *Moltke* and *Von der Tann*.

During the run southward the light and visibility favoured the German squadron and the British suffered accordingly. They also received a substantial shock when first *Indefatigable* and then *Queen Mary* suffered magazine explosions resulting in them sinking very rapidly and with heavy loss of life. On the appearance of the main German fleet Beatty turned his ships northward, in order both to escape and to reverse the previous situation and draw the enemy fleet onto the guns of the Grand Fleet. By this time the light was less favourable to the Germans, and the British battlecruisers (but not the 5th Battle Squadron which came under heavy fire from the German main fleet) faired better while Hipper's ships began to suffer more severely.

In the meantime the 3rd Battlecruiser Squadron had proceeded ahead of the Grand Fleet with the intention of rejoining Beatty and arrived to the north east of the scene of action. Hipper thus found himself between Beatty on the port bow and the 3rd Battlecruiser Squadron on his starboard bow. Correctly assuming that this new enemy was the vanguard of the British fleet, he hauled round to starboard to retire on his own main fleet and soon found himself in action with Hood's battlecruisers. Initially the British ships were very effective but after only twelve minutes in action the *Invincible* also blew up and sank. This effectively ended the major part of the battlecruisers' involvement in Jutland although they continued in intermittent action for the remainder of the day. The loss of three of their number under such appalling circumstances produced a strong reaction against the type, or at least against the type as conceived by Admiral Fisher. In the interim report of the Battlecruiser Fleet's post-Jutland Committee on Construction the following passage appears:

> The Committee consider that British battle cruisers, whether in service or about to be commissioned, are unequal to the duties assigned to them, as their protection is insufficient to enable them to encounter the capital ships of the enemy without incurring undue risk of destruction.
>
> For these duties the Committee are of opinion that vessels of very great protection, offensive power and speed are requisite; and that having regard to the existing naval situation and to the latest known foreign construction, the vessel required must be of fast battleship type, rather than on the lines of a battle cruiser. The 'Queen Elizabeth' type appears more nearly to fulfil the conditions required than does any other; but higher speed, greater protection and greater offensive power should be attempted, in conjunction, perhaps, with draught diminished to reduce under water target.

This sums up the opinion of the time and much of the opinion expressed since but, regardless of the value of the battlecruiser as a type, their failings were not simply a question of insufficient protection as, hopefully, this book will serve to make clear.

Origins

The *Invincible* had a totally different genesis from the *Dreadnought*. She was designed in order to meet a want that had long been felt but never supplied, namely, a ship fast enough to hunt down any armed merchant ship afloat, and at the same time to be able to fight any cruiser afloat. The word 'fight' with Fisher meant 'to crush'. With him there was no question of designing a cruiser *equal* in strength or speed to that of the enemy; for then the result of an action might be uncertain. His contention was that we should be superior to the enemy in numbers, in guns, in hitting power, in speed, and in personnel; and then, and only then, could the people of this country sleep peacefully in their beds.
(Admiral Sir R Bacon, *The Life of Lord Fisher of Kilverstone*, 1929)

Fisher's introduction of the battlecruiser type was open to more severe criticism [than the dreadnought battleship], because it fulfilled no real strategic nor tactical need. The statement that it was required to hunt down German liners is absurd. Trade has never been protected by hunting down raiders in the great ocean spaces, but if it were, the task could be performed more effectively by smaller cruisers costing less than half the price of a battlecruiser.
(Vice-Admiral K G B Dewar, *The Navy From Within*, 1939)

On 20 October 1904, Admiral Sir John Fisher became First Sea Lord of the Admiralty. He came to his new post armed with radical plans to modernise and reform the Royal Navy's organisation, training and material with the intention of improving its efficiency both in terms of readiness for war and financial economy. Although our primary concern here is with the most controversial of his material reforms – the introduction of the battlecruiser – it is necessary to have some understanding of Fisher himself and of contemporary battleship development before the evolution of the type can be fully understood.

Admiral Bacon, commenting on Fisher's practices, wrote that 'Every officer with ideas was consulted and their views assimilated, till Sir John became the embodiment of the advanced ideas of all classes of officers of the Fleet.'[1] In essence Fisher gathered together the ideas of others, combined them with his own and then campaigned for the adoption of the result. This process was developed and refined over a number of years, his plans being modified as necessary to accommodate changing circumstances, new developments in

technology and, occasionally, adverse comment on their feasibility. Whilst C-in-C Mediterranean Fleet, during 1899-1902, Fisher made a practice of giving lectures to its officers and it was from his notes on these that he began to organise a collection of papers which detailed his intended reforms. These were printed late in 1904 as the first iteration of *Naval Necessities*. In these papers, and in many of his letters of the period, it is possible to trace the above-mentioned process although never with absolute clarity. Fisher promoted his ideas with great passion and communicated these with a mixture of logical thought and simplistic dogma. It is difficult to tell how much of this was a true reflection of Fisher's thoughts and how much was intended as propaganda to persuade his reader or listener that his ideas were the obvious and logical answer to the Navy's future development. Large sections of these papers were written or inspired by others, principally those officers whom he regarded highly and upon whose advice he relied – particularly with regard to technical and tactical matters in which areas Fisher was less than fully competent, despite his background as a gunnery officer and fleet commander. Among his closest advisers were Captains John Jellicoe, Reginald Bacon, Henry Jackson and Charles Madden (all technical officers of considerable talent destined for high office – with or without Fisher's patronage), Constructor W H Gard of the DNC's department and the marine engineer Alexander Gracie of the Fairfield Shipbuilding Co. He also counted amongst his close friends Sir Philip Watts (DNC 1902-12) and Sir Andrew Noble (head of the Armstrong Whitworth shipbuilding and

The very large protected cruiser *Terrible* in 1899. She and her sister, *Powerful*, displaced 14,200 tons which was only slightly less than that of the contemporary battleships of the *Majestic* class and considerably greater than other British cruisers then in existence. The increased size was necessary to accommodate a large machinery installation for a speed of 22kts, at a time when the standard maximum speed for British First Class cruisers was 20kts. Both vessels were designed and built during the time of Fisher's period as Controller (1892-97). (Author's collection) armaments company) which gave him direct access to the latest thinking in warship design and weapon development.

For the majority of the time Fisher was absolutely convinced that he was right and one of his greatest talents was his ability to convince others to the same view. At a time when the Navy was conservatively approaching momentous changes in naval technology, he provided the focus and the inspiration required to move the Navy forward and to get things done efficiently and quickly. History has judged him a great leader because he was more often right than wrong. In part this was due to the fact that he never had absolute power – even as First Sea Lord he needed the support of his fellow officers and was answerable to his political masters – and this prevented many of his wilder schemes being put into effect. It should be added, however, that this also slowed the introduction of some of his more worthwhile ideas.

Fisher was quick to see the advantages of new developments in technology but slow to appreciate the disadvantages and limitations that usually accompanied them. He has often been described as a visionary because of his early and enthusiastic promotion of such innovations as the steam turbine, diesel engines, water tube and oil-fired boilers and submarines, but he tended to do this with *all* new developments and more often than not his predictions were somewhat less than accurate. The turbine did revolutionise warship propulsion but the diesel engine (submarines excepted) did not; oil-fired boilers were an immediate success but water tube boilers took some time to fulfil their initial promise; the submarine eventually became a very potent weapon but did not render the battleship obsolete. It is worth noting also that Fisher was far from alone in the promotion of new technologies, although the majority of those who were most enthusiastic were younger officers (who had limited ability to influence Admiralty policy) and it was from the brightest of these that Fisher formed his group of close advisers.

In his proposals for improved warship designs Fisher had an unwavering, almost obsessive, desire for high speed or, more exactly, a substantial excess of speed over foreign warships of equivalent type. In simple terms this was a perfectly logical requirement for which he argued in the following terms:

> The Battleships must be large because they must be fast; they must be fast because we want to take the offensive, and also because speed is both the principal tactical as well as the principal strategical factor. Superiority of speed corresponds to the 'weather gauge' of the old sailing days. It permits you to decline or to bring on an action. It enables you to anticipate the strategic dispositions of the enemy. It affords the necessary scope for endless schemes for enticing and entrapping the enemy. It makes your economic speed of a higher ratio.[2]

Fisher was, however, overestimating the tactical advantages of speed and made the critical mistake of assuming the enemy would not possess ships of equivalent speed. As any country embarking on challenging Britain's naval power would have to design ships capable of representing a serious threat, it followed that any escalation in the power of warships could ultimately lead to a technological naval race. There is the possible alternative, although not to my knowledge ever expressed by Fisher, of a deliberate escalating of naval development as a means of dissuading any challenge to Britain's naval supremacy. At the turn of the century most of Britain's potential rivals were military powers with large standing armies and limited desires to become involved in an escalating and expensive naval race with Britain and, like many others in the service, Fisher saw few problems in Britain continuing to maintain her supposed technological lead provided the country continued to see Britain's primary defence as on the sea. This view was reinforced by Britain's long naval tradition and the efficiency of her warship construction organisation. Unfortunately, it also tended to produce an arrogant belief in the superiority of British material which limited (along with financial restraints) critical appraisal of ships and their equipment prior to the First World War.

As acknowledged above, speed could be bought with increased size but this was limited by docking facilities and financial restraints. Britain's battleships already tended to be larger than their foreign contemporaries and there was strong political resistance to increases in the size, and therefore cost, of these vessels. Ultimately Fisher did, in instigating the dreadnought type, obtain sanction for larger ships but they were still required to be within certain limits and were only accepted on the understanding that there would be a compensatory overall saving in the Naval Estimates. However, Fisher also understood that speed could be obtained by modifying the balance of a design. In January 1901 he gave his requirements as firstly speed and secondly gunpower while '*the obligatory limit entailed by docking capabilities must curtail the other features in the design*, such as protection, amount of stores and provisions, etc . . . So in the internal arrangements, sacrifices must now be made to get our requirements within docking dimensions (not before this time compulsory), and there must be ruthless pruning of all accessories.'[3]

The first records of Fisher's development of a new approach in warship design date from early 1900 and by the summer of 1901 at the latest, he was communicating these ideas to the Admiralty. In December 1900 he suggested that new battleships should be larger than proposed French ships of 14,865 tons and should have a speed of 19kts if the French went to 18.5kts.[4] This is hardly a vast margin of speed (particularly as the French vessels in question proved to be 19kt vessels), but this requirement was soon to increase to 21kts. In his 'Rough Headings of 6th Lecture' (to the Mediterranean Fleet) dated 30 December 1901 he stated:

> The question of armament is all important! If we have the advantage of speed, *which is the first desideratum in every class of fighting vessel (Battleships included), then, and then only*, can we choose our distance for fighting. If we can choose our distance for fighting, then we can choose our armament for fighting! But how in the past has the armament been chosen? Do we arrange the armament to meet [the] proposed mode of fighting? Doesn't it sometimes look like so many of each sort as if you were peopling the Ark, and wanted representatives of all calibres?
>
> Now the armament we require is the greatest number of the largest quick-firing guns in *protected positions*. They call it the *secondary* armament; it is really the *primary* armament!
>
> In these days of very rapid movement the huge gun firing (comparatively) *slowly* is as obsolete as the foot soldier in the Boer War!
>
> **Whoever hits soonest and oftenest will win!**
>
> By many, a 10-inch gun (of the newest type and, say, 3300 feet [per second] initial velocity) is preferred to those of larger calibre. Why? Because it admits of so much more rapid firing; there is said to be a 10-inch gun now feasible which would be practically a quick-firer, and all the weights involved admit of hand working if the mechanism or electro-motors fail, where in these respects the heavier calibre would offer great difficulties.
>
> . . . So the problem is to fix the smallest large gun to put at each end of the ship, and the largest small quick-firing gun to put elsewhere with the largest arc of fire and the best view.[5]

Fisher's requirement for a reduction of the main armament calibre from 12in to 10in was based on the fact that the 12in guns of the 1890s were slow, ponderous weapons. Although their projectiles were heavier and potentially more damaging, the number of hits they might achieve, particularly at long range, compared badly with a lighter, faster-firing weapon that was easier to control.[6] His proposal for the 'largest small quick-firing gun' was the 7.5in, the increase from the standard 6in weapon being (a) to achieve improved accuracy at long range, (b) to compensate for a general increase in the thickness of medium armour in foreign ships, and (c) to increase hitting power. His great attachment to quick-firing guns resulted from their ability to smother a target in shells in a short space of time and thereby seriously reduce the

The battleship *Swiftsure* and her sister *Triumph*, under construction for Chile by Armstrong's and Vickers respectively, were purchased by the British Government in 1903 to prevent their purchase by Russia. They closely approximated to Fisher's ideal, being armed with four 10in and fourteen 7.5in guns, lightly protected and of comparatively high speed (20kts). (Author's collection)

enemy's secondary and minor armament, command and control positions, and signalling abilities.

These requirements were evolved in part from a series of interwoven developments and ideas related to progress in long-range gunnery and fire control. The French had begun serious work on the latter in the early 1890s and by 1897, when the generally accepted fighting range was about 1000yds to 2000yds, had carried out successful long-range firing trials at up to 4000yds.[7] In 1901 Fisher mentioned that 'Two Italian Admirals informed us last year that, following French practice, it was their intention to open fire at 7000 yards, as excellent results had been obtained by themselves and the French at that range, and though some ammunition would be wasted, yet the chance of a lucky shot . . . and the moral effect of commencing the action together with avoiding the demoralising effect of being fired at without firing back, all united to extend the practice of long-range firing, especially as the increased rapidity of firing in recent quick-firing systems enables the range to be quickly obtained.'[8] The latter remark refers to a method, initiated by the French, of using a QF gun to find the range by deliberately firing short and then progressively increasing the elevation of the gun until the target was straddled (a method which could not be employed with slow-firing weapons like the 12in gun). The British had begun experiments with long-range fire in the Mediterranean shortly before Fisher became C-in-C and by 1902 6000yds was generally accepted as the range for opening fire. Initially this was seen as a means of (a) inflicting damage on an enemy during the early stages of an action before closing to the fighting range of 3000 to 4000yds, and (b) to allow ships at long range to support other vessels more closely engaged with the enemy. However, as early as 1901 Fisher was predicting a fighting range of 6000yds and planned to use the gunnery exercises of the following year to establish what percentage of hits could be expected at different ranges. Within a few years practices were being carried out at 8000yds, and 5000yds to 6000yds was the expected fighting range. At this range, however, more sophisticated fire control techniques were necessary and during the period from 1902 to 1905 a great deal of effort was put into improving the method of controlling guns by both improving the gun mountings and in providing rangefinding, control and communication instruments.

One of the principal driving forces behind the need to extend the fighting range was a substantial improvement in the accuracy of the torpedo. Until the mid-1890s torpedoes were limited to short-range attack largely because they could not maintain a reasonably straight course for any distance. By 1898 this had been corrected by providing the torpedo with gyroscopic stabilisation which gave a remarkable reduction in 'deviation' (drift away from the line of fire) and made the development of longer-range torpedoes worthy of consideration. It was also a relatively cheap innovation and could be applied without difficulty to existing torpedoes. In 1898 the longest standard range settings for the most recent British 18in torpedo was 800yds. By 1902 this had increased to 2000yds and there were prospects of even greater increases in the near future. Under these circumstances increased gun range was essential but even here Fisher managed to get in his requirement for speed: 'Thus the employment of the gyroscope makes it imperative [that] we should never close the enemy within 2000 yards *or 3000 yards if pursuing! This, however, infers superiority of speed, especially for the Battleships.*'[9]

Early in 1900 Bacon submitted a paper to Fisher pointing out that the advent of long-range gunnery favoured single line formation for the tactical employment of the battlefleet. Up to this time naval tacticians had favoured the use of semi-independent squadrons to break up an enemy fleet by 'concentration of force', a method which lent itself to short ranges and the mobility provided by steam propulsion but which also led to some very complex systems of fleet manoeuvre and control. Bacon argued that line-ahead maximised available gunfire, ensured clear arcs of fire and gave 'the greatest flexibility and simplicity of manoeuvre.' He added that as the gun was the primary weapon 'the best tactics were those that gave the gun the fullest possible scope. Gyrations which upset gun pointing were obviously bad, and therefore the advantages of the single line became even more apparent.' He added that under these conditions a faster fleet would have advantages and outlined much the same tactical arguments for speed in battle as those subsequently used by Fisher (see above).[10]

Fisher seems to have accepted the line-ahead formation with some reluctance for although he advocated its use – and employed Bacon's arguments often – he also recorded the comment that 'The British Navy is armed at present for broadside fighting; it may be a matter for regret but there is the fact that it is so.'[11] He thus accepted it as a *fait accompli* resulting from the design of ships rather than a matter of choice resulting from tactical thought. It seems probable that this prompted his advocacy of ships designed to give 'equal fire all-round' in order to restore mobility of action, concentration of force, etc. Unfortunately, ships do not lend themselves to a suitable distribution of armament to achieve this end and most of the capital ships of the early Dreadnought period were compromised to some extent by an excessive emphasis on end-on fire. It is worth noting that fire-control is also much more difficult end-on than on the broadside particularly if a ship is rolling. One interesting point made by Bacon was that 'Mobility was useless without considerable excess of speed' and it is hardly likely that Fisher did not take note of what he would certainly consider a statement of great significance.

The armoured cruiser

During the 1890s the armoured cruiser became a very popular type among the world's navies. These were large vessels – usually approaching the size of contemporary battleships – of high speed and armed with QF guns. They came close to supplanting the construction of other, smaller, cruiser types but had the disadvantage of being exceedingly costly and could not therefore be built in the numbers required by a colonial power like Britain. They were 'armoured' as opposed to 'protected' because their primary passive defence was vertical side armour as opposed to an arched steel deck and were consequently much more capable of withstanding attack from QF guns. Britain began to build vessels of this type somewhat later than other countries. Between 1897 and 1901 four classes

Table 1: White's armoured cruisers

Class	Design year	Completion	No of ships	Displacement (tons)	Armament	Speed (kts)	Belt armour KC(ins)
Cressy	1897	1901-02	6	12,000	2 × 9.2in, 12 × 6in	21	6
Drake	1898	1902-03	4	14,150	2 × 9.2in, 16 × 6in	23	6
Monmouth	1899	1903-04	10	9800	14 × 6in	23	4
Devonshire	1901	1905	6	10,850	4 × 7.5in, 6 × 6in	22	6

A typical armoured cruiser of the White era, *Essex* of the *Monmouth* class seen here in 1913. Note the 6in casemate guns on the broadside. (Author's collection)

One of the armoured cruisers designed under the direction of Sir Philip Watts, *Cochrane* of the *Warrior* class. Note that all the main armament is mounted in single turrets, two 9.2in on the centreline forward and aft, and two 9.2in and two 7.5in on each broadside. (Author's collection)

(totalling twenty-six ships) were designed under the direction of the DNC, Sir William White (see Table 1) the first entering service in 1901. They all had turret mountings fore and aft – single 9.2in in the *Cressy* and *Drake*, twin 6in in the *Monmouth* and single 7.5in in the *Devonshire*. The latter class also had a single 7.5in turret on each side abreast the bridge. The remaining 6in guns in all these ships were mounted in broadside casemates.

Fisher was much impressed by large cruisers in general and the armoured cruiser in particular, although not necessarily with White's interpretation. In particular he would have regarded the two *County* classes as too small and did not care for casemate-mounted guns. He much preferred an all-turret armament, each turret being a well-protected, self-contained unit with its own ammunition supply. This was intended to provide for the improved survivability of the guns and reduce the dangers inherent in extended ammunition supply routes via ammunition passages which were particularly vulnerable to torpedo attack (and, as it

Table 2: Watts' armoured cruisers

Class	Design year	Completion	No of ships	Displacement (tons)	Armament	Speed (kts)	Belt armour KC(ins)
Duke of Edinburgh	1902	1906	2	13,550	6 × 9.2in, 10 × 6in	23	6
Warrior	1903	1906-07	4	13,550	6 × 9.2in, 4 × 7.5in	23	6
Minotaur	1904	1908-09	3	14,600	4 × 9.2in, 10 × 7.5in	23	6

turned out, long-range gunfire). It also served to reduce the number of personnel involved in passing ammunition. In addition Fisher was much against unnecessary superstructure which might serve to detonate shells and White's ships carried substantial superfluous (for fighting purposes) structure above the upper deck. There was a marked change in approach when Philip Watts succeeded White as DNC in 1902. Under Watts direction three further armoured cruiser classes were designed (see Table 2), all of substantial size, with considerably reduced superstructure and, with the exception of the first two ships, which had ten 6in guns in casemates, an all-turret mounted armament. They could, however, still be criticised for poor ammunition supply arrangements and by the time they were under construction Fisher had concluded that their speed of 23kts was insufficient.

There was another class of vessel to which Fisher was very much attached. This was the Second Class battleship, of which there were several examples in the British and other navies. Generally these were more lightly armed and protected than First Class battleships and slightly faster. Fisher's particular favourite was *Renown* which had been designed and built during his term at the Admiralty as Controller (1891-97) and had served as his flagship when C-in-C of the North America and West Indies Station (1897-99) and in the Mediterranean (1899-1902). The particulars of this ship are given in Table 3 – her light armament and relatively light armour are worthy of note. She was not only faster than the contemporary First Class battleships of the *Majestic* class but in heavy weather she was, because of her size, capable of overhauling a cruiser.

In 1901 Fisher was proposing much the same armament for his ideal armoured cruiser as he was for battleships and was indicating that the armour in the latter should be reduced to improve speed. This effectively blurred the distinction between the two types and seems to have caused Fisher to develop the notion that the armoured cruiser could replace the battleship; or more correctly that the two types should be merged since the new type would automatically have become the prime unit of the fleet. In December 1900 he described the latest French armoured cruisers as 'battleships in disguise', a phrase he was to use often during the next few years in describing his armoured cruiser proposals. He also often referred to his fast battleship designs (and to *Renown*) as 'glorified armoured cruisers'. At times he seems to have become somewhat confused as to which type, battleship or armoured cruiser, should be developed and occasionally made incompatible statements on the subject within the same document. One suspects that, given subsequent events, he always had a strong personal preference for the armoured cruiser as the capital ship of the future but could find little support for this view

Table 3: HMS *Renown*

LAID DOWN:	1893
LAUNCHED:	1895
COMPLETED:	1897
DISPLACEMENT:	12,350 tons
SPEED	18kts
ARMAMENT:	4 × 10in/40cal (2 × 2)
	10 × 6in (10 × 1)
	12 × 12pdr (12 × 1)
ARMOUR:	Main belt 8in; upper belt 6in; bulkheads 10in and 6in; casemates 6in-4in; CT 10in; deck 2in-3in

among his contemporaries and was therefore forced to accept the battleship as a necessary part of any future programme. Initially his view was not entirely insupportable given the proposed armament of QF guns and the expectation that actions would be fought at long range (both of which allowed for thinner armour) but with the subsequent readoption of the heavy calibre gun it is difficult to understand why he continued to advocate high speed at the expense of protection.

At the beginning of 1902 Fisher enlisted the help of W H Gard, then Chief Constructor at Malta, to produce an outline design to meet his requirements for a 25kt armoured cruiser. The result, which Fisher christened HMS *Perfection*, had the following outline particulars:

Displacement: 15,000 tons (14,000 tons with oil-fired boilers)
Dimensions: 500ft (min) × 70ft (min) × 26ft 6in (mean)
Armament: 4 × 9.2in (2 × 2); 12 × 7.5in QF (6 × 2)
Machinery: 35,000ihp (max) = 25kts
Protection: 6in-5in side; 6in bulkheads; 6in on 9.2in mountings; 4in on 7.5in mountings; 10in CT; 2in upper deck; 2.5in (for), 2.5–3in (aft) lower deck.

He wrote to the First Lord, Selborne, in March 1902 stating that he had this design 'ready for May [Rear-Admiral W H May – Controller 1901-04] and Watts' and outlined its general features including the facts that she would be able to fire ten guns ahead and astern; had an all-turret armament, each turret being a self-contained unit; no masts, derricks, anchor gear or bridges; linoleum-covered decks instead of wood planking; and telescopic funnels. The last item, one of Fisher's constant favourites, was intended (a) to reduce the target in action, and (b) limit the observabilty of the ship when scouting – how it intended to cope with the smoke is not recorded. This proposal had little effect on Admiralty construction policy. The only similarities between this vessel and the armoured cruisers designed in the following two years was an increase in the calibre of the secondary armament, a reduction in top hamper and an all-turret armament – all items which resulted from

Table 4: Particulars of ships employed in Senior Officers' War Course, January 1902

	Type A Heavily-armed battleship	Type B Lightly-armed battleship
DEEP DISPLACEMENT:	17,604 tons	15,959 tons
SPEED AT LOAD DRAUGHT:	18kts	22kts
ARMAMENT:	4 × 12in (2 × 2); 8 × 8in (4 × 2); 12 × 7in (7 × 1)	4 × 10in (2 × 2); 16 × 6in (16 × 1)
ARMOUR:	10-8in belt; 6in upper belt; 11in main armament; 8in intermediate armament; 7in secondary armament; 1.5in deck	6in belt; 5in upper belt; 9.5in main armament; 5in secondary armament

decisions emanating primarily from Watts and May.

In June 1902 Fisher left the Mediterranean to take up the post of Second Sea Lord at the Admiralty where, if he was not aware of it already, he would soon have discovered that battleship design was moving in a quite different direction to that proposed by him from the Mediterranean. Rear-Admiral May had begun a detailed study of the requirements for future armoured ships in light of recent developments in naval construction abroad (particularly in the USA[12]) and in naval gunnery. The conclusions ultimately reached were that the heavy-calibre gun was of primary importance, that the secondary armament needed to be increased in calibre (to cope with increased ranges and the thicker armour in foreign designs) and that protection needed to be both thicker and more widely distributed. In effect British ships were to be individually superior to their foreign contemporaries and this in turn meant an increase in size. Under the direction of Watts design work on battleships to meet these criteria began in 1902 and resulted in the *Lord Nelson* and *Agamemnon* – the last, largest and most powerfully armed and armoured of Britain's pre-dreadnoughts which retained the then standard speed for British vessels of this type of 18kts.[13]

In January 1902, almost certainly as part of the above investigation and possibly because of Fisher's prompting, the Admiralty requested the Senior Officers' War Course at Greenwich Naval College to investigate whether a lightly armed and protected ship with a 4kt advantage in speed had any tactical advantage over a vessel in which speed was subordinated to gun power and armour. The officer in charge of the course, Captain H J May, concluded in his report, completed on 8 February 1902, that gun power was more important than speed provided both sides were determined to fight. The two ships employed in this investigation (see Table 4), despite being referred to only as 'Type A' and 'Type B' and both being described as battleships, were in fact the very latest US Navy designs for battleship and armoured cruiser respectively.[14] The proposed battle between the two types assumed that fire would be opened at 6000yds and the ships would then close, or attempt to close, to 4000yds and finally 3000yds. It was stated that the lightly-protected ship was more vulnerable to the fire

of her adversary, whose better-protected hull and primary gun positions made her immune at all ranges. However, three of the lighter type were considered capable of holding their own against two of the heavier type at long range, where their high rate of fire would help. 'It is evident, therefore, that the 'B' ship should so far as possible fight at long range, and that her speed should be used to prevent a heavier antagonist from closing. However close she gets her 6in guns will never become armour piercers. They must, therefore, be looked upon as purely shell guns when pitted against a well-protected modern ship.' It was also stated that the lighter vessel could use her speed to keep her distance in 'fighting a retiring action' but this would only be of use if the heavier ship wanted to chase. The paper concluded '. . . for fighting a fleet, the 'B' ships are much inferior to the 'A's. Their speed may be of the greatest moment strategically, but it is a well nigh negligible quantity tactically.'[15] In July 1902 the DNI, Captain R Custance, commented that this paper

. . . proved that the large armoured cruiser of 22 knots speed, costing upwards of a million sterling is not as efficient in the line of battle as a battleship of 18 knots, and as such a powerful ship should not be detached from the fleet, it is difficult to see how such a ship can be justified.

That enquiry into the strategic conditions may lead to results somewhat similar to those obtained from the investigation of the tactical conditions seems to be not unlikely.

Naval opinion has been and is now under the influence of the traditions of the Napoleonic wars, when we had such a superiority over the forces opposed to us that we were able to blockade them in their ports, and they were forced to evade us whenever they put to sea. We are deeply imbued with the conceit that the enemy must and will still evade us. This idea is a relic of the past, and is no longer fitted to the new conditions. We must look back to the Dutch Wars to find a precedent for the future – to conditions of equality when our supremacy at sea was disputed. No idea of evasion entered into the Dutch mind in the 17th Century, nor will it enter into the German or French mind in the 20th. Neither of these nations will go to war with us alone. We shall have to fight pitched battles to establish our supremacy, and, as Captain May and his officers have shown, these must be decided by fighting power without help from speed.[16]

Printed at the same time as the paper on the tactical value of speed was a series of notes by Captain May on the exercises and problems investigated at Greenwich.[17] Some of the conclusions in this document are particularly relevant and these are briefly summarised below.

Main Armament: The 12in gun was considered more useful than the QF gun at long and short ranges. Given its importance it was concluded that the tacticians task was to keep as many of these weapons bearing on the enemy as possible. To this end the ideal formation was in line-ahead with the enemy on the broadside.

QF Armament: This was of high value at medium ranges for piercing the armour of secondary batteries. However, a gun was required that could pierce 7in to 8in KC armour for which, as the 6in was outclassed and the 7.5in was borderline, the 9.2in QF gun was recommended.

Tactics: Although the ideal tactical manoeuvre was to cross ahead of an enemy fleet (crossing the 'T') this would be extremely difficult to achieve when fighting at long range as any attempt to move ahead of the enemy could be countered by a turn away. This would simply lead to the slower fleet turning inside the circle of the faster fleet at a radius proportional to the difference in speed.

Fisher seems to have been undeterred by these developments, although they no doubt served to modify at least some of his views. He could of course have argued that the armoured cruiser used in the War Course exercise did not meet his requirements for speed or armament. In any case, at this time he was heavily occupied, as Second Sea Lord, in developing new schemes of entry and training for officers and men. Nevertheless, his position on the Board would have kept him in touch with design developments. During this time the designs of the *Lord Nelson* and *Warrior* were being worked out and among the numerous sketch designs for the former were several with a uniform 10in gun armament (12in was also suggested by the DNC's department). It is easy to assume that the idea of the 10in calibre emanated from Fisher, as he no doubt found occasions on which to express his opinions, but it is difficult to tell who was influencing who, as Watts himself favoured the 10in gun as did his former employer, Noble. Besides, according to Bacon, Fisher kept his plans to himself while at the Admiralty to avoid the possibility of their being watered-down and only partially adopted.[18] It is

also doubtful that the Third Sea Lord would have looked kindly upon any direct interference with the departments under his control.

Fisher left the Admiralty in August 1903 to become C-in-C Portsmouth where he once more began detailed work on his plans to modernise the Navy prior to becoming First Sea Lord. On the material side he sought the help of his close advisers, two of whom – Gard (now Chief Constructor of Portsmouth Dockyard) and Bacon (serving as Inspecting Captain of Submarine Boats at Portsmouth) – were readily available.[19] The most notable difference between the armoured ship designs he now proposed and those of his period in the Mediterranean was the adoption of a uniform-calibre armament – sixteen 10in in the battleship and sixteen 9.2in in the armoured cruiser. Both vessels were to be of 15,900 tons, the battleship having a speed of 21kts and the armoured cruiser 25.5kts.

The uniform-calibre main armament resulted from recent developments in fire control where it had been found that salvo firing was the best means of controlling guns at long range. Unfortunately guns of differing calibre could not be controlled as a unit owing to the ballistic differences between them and the resulting variations in the sight settings required for different ranges and deflections. At the same time, attempting to control them as separate groups merely caused confusion, as it was almost impossible to distinguish the fall of shot of one group from another. The only answer to this problem was a uniform-calibre main armament which could be controlled as a single group. As a result of this change Fisher reinterpreted his requirement for the 'smallest big gun and the biggest small gun' as meaning that the only guns to be carried other than the uniform main armament were those of the anti-torpedo boat battery for which, at this time, he favoured the 4in calibre.

Outline designs for the proposed battleship and armoured cruiser, produced by Gard, were available before Fisher became First Sea Lord in October 1904. However, by this time a major shift had occurred in the requirements for the battleship as a result of arguments put forward by his naval advisors (particularly Bacon) regarding the calibre of the main armament. This again developed from the use of spotting for fire control which required that the fall of shot was registered before the next salvo was fired. Under these circumstances the rate of fire was not controlled by the rapidity with which the guns could be loaded but by the time of flight of the projectiles. This effectively negated one of the primary advantages of the 10in over the 12in gun – its higher rate of fire (in addition, the latest design of heavy gun mounting gave a much improved rate of fire). The 12in gun could also claim:

(a) Greater destructive effect of each hit due to heavier projectile and larger bursting charge.

Table 5: HMS *Unapproachable*, October 1904

DIMENSIONS:	530ft × 75ft × 26ft 6in
MACHINERY:	40,000ihp = 25.5kts at 110rpm
ENDURANCE:	2425nm at 25kts; 15680nm at 10kts
ARMAMENT:	16 × 9.2in (8 × 2); *c*12 × 4in
ARMOUR:	6in belt (8in at wing barbettes);
	8in barbettes
COAL:	2500 tons
OIL:	600 tons in double bottom

WEIGHTS (tons):		
Equipment	680	
Coal (normal)	1100	
Armament	1820 (incl gunhouses, torpedoes and stores)	
Prop machinery	3400	
Armour and backing	3000	
Hull	5000 (incl electric motors)	
TOTAL:	15,000 tons	

(b) Improved accuracy and smaller spread of salvo at long range.

(c) Flatter trajectory of projectile and hence greater danger space for target at long range.

Against this the 10in gun could claim lower cost of guns, mountings and ammunition, more economical use of weight for armour and the ability to provide greater numbers of guns on a given displacement.

The choice between a battleship armed with sixteen 10in guns and one armed with eight 12in guns appeared in Fisher's papers in the summer of 1904. In these he expressed the opinion that the arguments in favour of the 12in were 'unanswerable' but, nevertheless, kept the options open for discussion and the decision to adopt the 12in gun was not finalised until after he took up his seat on the Board. In the meantime the armoured cruiser design retained the 9.2in calibre armament and Gard's outline design for this vessel, known as HMS *Unapproachable* (see Table 5: the battleship was HMS *Untakable*), appeared in the papers submitted by Fisher to Selborne in October 1904. However, it seems alternatives *were* discussed as, in these same documents Fisher made the point that for the cruiser the 10in gun was not considered to have sufficient advantage over the 9.2in to justify the additional weight involved and the 12in gun was 'unnecessarily large'. Bacon has recorded that while Fisher's unofficial committee was in full agreement over the adoption of the heavy gun for the battleship, the armoured cruiser's armament was the subject of 'much controversy' and the discussion on the relative merits of the 9.2in and 12in gun continued 'for weeks'. Eventually the 12in gun 'won on the unanswerable plea that ships, of the size and tonnage necessary . . . should have an additional use in being able to form a fast light squadron to supplement the battleships in action, and worry the ships in the van or rear of the

enemy's line.'[20] The decision to adopt the 12in gun for both the battleship (soon to become HMS *Dreadnought*) and the armoured cruiser was formally taken at a meeting of the Board in December 1904 when the main features to be adopted were finally settled. In part, this may have emanated from a desire by Fisher to retain the similarity of armament of the two types in the hope of maintaining his arguments for replacing battleships altogether. Whatever the reasons, the decision to adopt the 12in gun for the armoured cruiser was critical – it was this, and this alone, that produced the distinct and separate warship type that was eventually to be classified as the battlecruiser. Had the 9.2in calibre been retained the resulting vessels would have been simply a major advance in the evolution of the armoured cruiser in the same way as the *Dreadnought* was a major advance in the evolution of the battleship.

The functions for the big-gun armoured cruisers were essentially the same as those of existing armoured cruisers, the additional speed and gun power being seen as enhancing their effectiveness in these roles. In summary these were:

(a) *To provide a heavy scouting force.* Because of their heavy armament they could push through any existing cruiser screen and report on the composition of an enemy fleet by close observation, following which their speed enabled a rapid retirement. It was assumed that, as their approach and retirement would be end-on, their protection would be sufficient to get reasonably close to an enemy battlefleet, their armour, for most of the time, only be subjected to oblique attack.

(b) *Close support for the battlefleet in action.* They were to be stationed in the van and rear of the battle line where they could defend the battleships against interference by enemy cruisers and worry the enemy battleships with their big guns as opportunity offered. In the latter case they were only to engage battleships already fully occupied in fighting their opposite numbers (it was unlikely in these circumstances that a battleship would shift its fire to the lesser of two dangers). They could also operate as a fast wing and attempt to outmanoeuvre the enemy by enveloping movements across the van or rear of his line – again if opportunity offered and the enemy battleships were otherwise occupied.

(c) *In pursuit of a fleeing enemy.* In a chasing action they were to use their speed and gun power to harass the retiring enemy fleet in the hope of damaging and slowing their ships.

(d) *Trade protection.* To hunt down and destroy enemy surface raiding cruisers and armed merchantmen. Speed was seen as essential for this function, both to give some margin over the likely enemy vessels and in order to reach the area of operations quickly. End-on fire was also of importance in this role as chasing actions would be the norm.

The Committee on Designs

The radical nature of the proposed shipbuilding policy (which also included destroyers and submarines but no intermediate types of cruiser at all) was such as to guarantee controversy. In consequence Fisher and the Board decided to appoint a 'Committee on Designs' ostensibly to investigate and report upon the requirements for future ships. However, its primary purpose was to validate decisions already arrived at and, because it was to consist of eminent and expert men whose opinions could not lightly be ignored, limit the level of criticism that could be aimed directly at the Board in general and Fisher in particular. The resulting Committee did valuable work at a detail level, in particular in sorting out the armament layout and main machinery to be used in the armoured ships, but it did not otherwise have any major influence on events. From the outset the basic requirements were those set by Fisher and he did not provide the Committee with any options to move outside the general parameters set by the Board of Admiralty. The Committee was officially appointed by Admiralty letter, dated 22 December 1904, and included all of Fisher's close advisers and several eminent civilians including the country's leading physicist, Lord Kelvin, and the superintendent of the Admiralty Experiment Works, R E Froude. Fisher himself acted as President of the Committee.[21]

At the first meeting of the Committee, on 3 January 1905, Fisher read the terms of reference, which in simple form stated that the Committee was advisory only and did not relieve the DNC of his responsibility for warship design but was so constituted that the advice it offered to the Board would carry great weight. The instructions given to the Committee outlined the designs to be considered for the battleship, armoured cruiser and destroyers (submarines were not included in the Committee's brief). In the case of the armoured cruiser these were simply that it should be of 25.5kts speed, armed with 12in and anti-torpedo boat guns only, armoured on the same scale as *Minotaur* and of dimensions suitable for existing docking facilities. However, the Committee also adopted a preliminary statement which was essentially a reiteration of the arguments put forward in the 'Types of Fighting Vessels' section of *Naval Necessities*.[22] There was some additional material concerning recent events in the Russo-Japanese War (February 1904-September 1905) which were taken to confirm the value of the armoured cruiser, the heavy gun, uniform armament, speed and long-range gunfire.[23]

The Committee first considered the battleship designs and then moved on to the first, and at this time, only, armoured cruiser design. This was design 'A'

Table 6: Particulars of armoured cruisers with reciprocating engines considered by Committee on Designs, January 1905

	Design A	*Design B*	*Designs D & E*
DATE:	4/1/05	4/1/05	12/1/05
LENGTH pp (ft):	540	540	550
BEAM (ft-in):	77	77-6	79
DRAUGHT (ft-in):	26-6	26-6	26-6
DISPLACEMENT (tons):	17,000	17,200	17,750
WEIGHTS (tons):			
General equipment	640	640	640
Armament	2500	2500	2500
Machinery	3500	3500	3600
Coal	1000	1000	1000
Armour	3160	3260	3460
Hull	6100	6200	6450
BM	100	100	100
TOTAL:	17,000	17,200	17,750

Particulars common to all designs: Machinery 41,000hp (D & E 42,500) = 25.5kts; Armament 8 × 12in (80rpg), 13 (D & E 14) × 4in (200rpg), 2 × Maxims, 5 submerged torp tubes; Armour 6in & 4in (3in backing) side,   6in & 3in bulkheads, 8in barbettes, 8in gun shields, 10in (10in & 6in D and E) CT, 6in & 2in com tube, 1.5in & 2in lower deck.

The above design details are taken from the legends of the designs in the Ship's Cover of the *Invincible* class (ADM138/248). The details given with sketch designs D and E in the Design Committee's Progress Report (*Fisher Papers* Vol 1, pp285-290) do not match these in several respects and in all the designs the speed of 25kts is incorrect. It is possible that these figures were doctored and/or badly recorded some time after the designs were first presented. Unfortunately there was no legend for Design C in the Covers and the only figures available are those from the Committee's report which give the displacement as 15,600 tons and dimensions as 520 × 76 × 26ft. It can be fairly safely assumed that the speed was 25.5kts and that the common particulars given above also applied to this design (except that the main armament was six 12in).

which was prepared by Constructor C H Croxford on instructions from the DNC, via ADNC W H Whiting. The DNC provided a rough plan showing the layout required for the main armament which, on 28 December, was given as eight 12in/50cal (not 45cal as finally adopted) guns. The machinery was specified as turbines of 42,000hp for a speed of 25.5kts and protection as on the same scale as *Minotaur*. However, when Croxford received his instructions on the following day, the turbines had been replaced by reciprocating engines. It is worth noting that despite a claim by Bacon that 'By the 21st October the sketch designs of the *Dreadnought* and *Invincible* were practically complete, and . . . subsequently underwent very little alteration',[24] none of the sketch designs for the armoured cruiser emanated from Gard and the designs finally adopted, for both the battleship and the armoured cruiser, were produced entirely by the DNC's department after the above date.[25]

The primary requirement for the armoured cruiser layout was to secure good end-on fire and Design 'A' was arranged to allow for four guns firing ahead and astern and six on the broadside. The arrangement was rejected on the grounds that the superfiring turret aft would cause serious blast interference to the lower turret when firing on after bearings and that the after group of turrets represented a large target which one hit might put completely out of action. At a second meeting, in the afternoon, the DNC was requested to prepare two new sketch designs ('B' and 'C'), and to produce diagrams of blast curves for 12in and smaller guns. These he duly produced at the third meeting on 4 January. The blast diagram revealed that blast problems would also occur between 12in mountings arranged abreast, as in the two new designs, and these were rejected also. The weak broadside fire was also objected to, and it was pointed out that the considerable weight of two mountings and their protection mounted so far forward (and aft in 'B') was likely to have a serious effect on the ships' seagoing qualities

Table 7: Particulars of armoured cruisers with turbine machinery considered by Committee on Designs, January 1905

	Design E	*Design D & E*	
DATE:	18/1/05	21/1/05	
LENGTH (ft):	530	540* (525**)	
BEAM (ft):	79	79	
DRAUGHT (ft):	26	26	
SPEED (kts):	25.5	25.5	

Armament and armour as reciprocating engine designs (Table 6)

WEIGHTS (tons):			
General equipment	620	620*	600**
Armament	2530	2500	2500
Machinery	2350	3140	2350
Coal	1000	1000	1000
Armour	3350	3370	3300
Hull	6050	6120	5850
BM	100	100	100
TOTAL:	16,000	16,850	15,700

* Assumes 12.5 per cent saving and ** assumes 30 per cent saving on machinery weight. The comparative Design E, with reciprocating engines, of 18 January was the same as that of 12 January except for a reduction in the power of the machinery (42,000hp) and in some slight adjustments of weight (displacement 17,600 tons – later modified by Whiting to 17,850 tons).

Table 8: Evolution of Design E, February 1905

DATE:	10/2/05*	10/2/05**	22/2/05***	22/2/05****
LENGTH (ft):	540	530	540	540
BEAM (ft):	79	79	79	79
DRAUGHT (ft):	26	26	26	26
DISPLACEMENT (tons):	16,750	16,000	16,750	16,750
SPEED (kts):	25.5	25.5	25	25
WEIGHTS (tons):				
General equipment	720	720	720	720
Armament	2470	2470	2450	2420
Machinery	2950	2350	3090	3090
Coal	1000	1000	1000	1000
Armour	3460	3410	3390	3420
Hull	6050	5950	6000	6000
BM	100	100	100	100
TOTAL:	16,750	16,000	16,750	16,750

* Assumes 15 per cent saving on machinery weight by use of turbines.
** Assumes 33 per cent saving on machinery weight by use of turbines.
*** Version 'A' – without magazine protection.
**** Version 'B' – with magazine protection.
Other particulars were as in the previous legends of 'E' except for the changes to protection in Version 'B', as detailed in the text, and the ATB armament which was 17 × 12pdr (300rpg) in the designs of 10 February and 20 × 12pdr (300rpg) in those of 22 February.

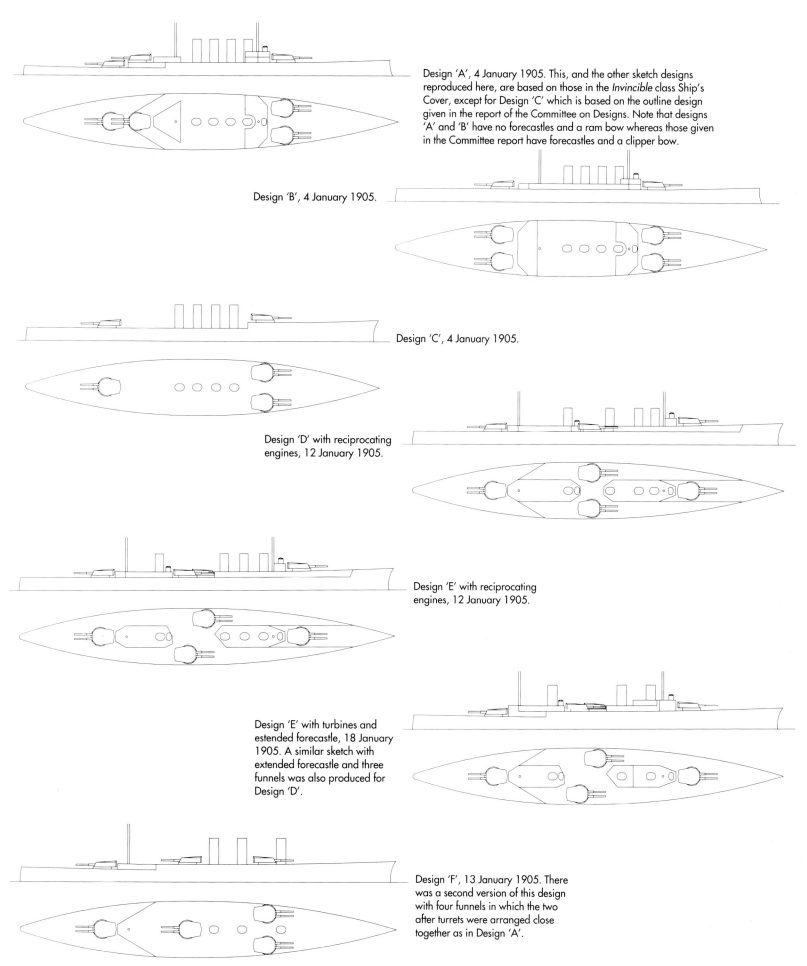

Design 'A', 4 January 1905. This, and the other sketch designs reproduced here, are based on those in the *Invincible* class Ship's Cover, except for Design 'C' which is based on the outline design given in the report of the Committee on Designs. Note that designs 'A' and 'B' have no forecastles and a ram bow whereas those given in the Committee report have forecastles and a clipper bow.

Design 'B', 4 January 1905.

Design 'C', 4 January 1905.

Design 'D' with reciprocating engines, 12 January 1905.

Design 'E' with reciprocating engines, 12 January 1905.

Design 'E' with turbines and extended forecastle, 18 January 1905. A similar sketch with extended forecastle and three funnels was also produced for Design 'D'.

Design 'F', 13 January 1905. There was a second version of this design with four funnels in which the two after turrets were arranged close together as in Design 'A'.

Fisher's favourite flagship, the Second Class battleship *Renown*. (Author's collection)

due to the excessive pitching that would probably result. It was decided that some wider distribution of the 12in turrets was required which would secure both end-on and broadside fire but reduce blast effects to an acceptable level. The proposal finally adopted was to place one turret forward, one aft and one on each beam giving a broadside of six guns and the ability to fire four guns on forward and after bearings (six on a very limited arc directly fore and aft). This decision resulted in the production of designs 'D' and 'E' which Croxford prepared for the next meeting on 12 January. Design 'E' differed from 'D' only in that the beam turrets were displaced *en echelon* to allow cross-deck firing over a limited arc of fire which, because of the blast effects, was only to be employed if the opposite turret was out of action. The Committee decided they preferred 'E' but asked for the forecastle to be lengthened as far as the after turret, to improve seaworthiness and to give the wing turrets a higher command. Although it was decided to work out this design in greater detail the Committee discussed one further alternative layout. This was design 'F', a variation on 'A' in which the two forward turrets were moved aft to wing positions abreast the forward funnels and the third turret was moved forward to a position between the engine and boiler rooms (basically the same layout as that adopted for the battleship but with the fore turret omitted). Croxford provided sketch layouts for this on the day of the meeting but at the Fifth meeting on the following day, at which only the Admiralty members of the Committee were present, it was decided not to proceed with this design, 'E' becoming the accepted layout for the new ships.

On 7 January the DNC mentioned that a four-shaft turbine arrangement might be adopted and Croxford was requested to produce alternative versions of 'D' and 'E' with this machinery.[26] The sketch designs for these were virtually identical to those of the reciprocating versions except, because they required less boiler power, they had three funnels instead of four. A preliminary discussion on the turbine took place during the 'Admiralty only' meeting on 13 January. Both the DNC and E-in-C urged their adoption on the basis of their simplicity, reliability and because of the great saving in weight that would result. However, several of the naval officers were concerned about the possible loss of manoeuvrability and astern power that was likely to be caused by the use of small, high-speed propellers. On 17 January evidence was taken from Sir Charles Parsons (British inventor of the turbine) and on the following day, when the comparative legends of design 'E' with turbines and reciprocating engines were available, the Committee decided to recommend the adoption of design 'E' with turbines, provided further investigation did not reveal any reason to reverse this decision. This debate, which continued for several weeks, included taking further evidence from Parsons and a detailed examination of the qualities of existing turbine-driven ships. Eventually it was concluded that the advantages far outweighed any disadvantage that might result (see also Machinery chapter).

One further major advance remained to be included in the design – defence against mines and torpedoes. This question had been brought to the fore as a result of recent events in the Russo-Japanese War where losses from mines were heavy. The principle concern was the vulnerability of magazines and in designs 'D' and 'E' provision was made to keep these as near the middle-line, and as far away from the ship's sides as possible. Consideration was also given to providing some form of armoured screen to the magazines and shell rooms. This eventually led to the incorporation of 2.5in-thick internal protective bulkheads abreast these compartments. This innovation was discussed by the Admiralty members of the Committee on 21 February. On the following day comparative legends for design 'E', with and without these bulkheads (version 'A' and 'B' respectively) were placed before the full Committee. To accommodate the additional 250 tons required for these bulkheads without increasing the overall displacement the 'B' version had been modified as follows:

(a) Height of belt armour above the load water line reduced from 7ft 3in to 6ft 9in (the original height was restored in the final legend of June 1905).
(b) 50ft of forward 4in side armour reduced in thickness to 3in.
(c) Sides of 12in gun shields reduced from 8in to 7in.
(d) Barbette armour reduced from 8in to 7in.
(e) Height of axis of forward 12in guns reduced from 34ft to 32ft above load water line.

The Committee approved these changes, except that item (b) was replaced by an alternative suggestion to reduce the heights of the guns' axis of the wing turrets from 29ft 6in to 28ft 6in (subsequently further reduced to 28ft). It was with these legends that the speed dropped from 25.5kts to 25kts. No explanation was offered but it seems likely that the extra 0.5kt could not be guaranteed on the proposed displacement and an increase in the latter for so small a gain in speed was not considered worthwhile.

The 22 February gathering was effectively the Committee's final meeting although various subcommittees (with all naval members) were formed to discuss various details of the designs. Despite this, the report they approved on this day was described as the *First Progress Report*. To the best of the author's knowledge no further full report was ever produced and one cannot help but feel that at this point in the proceedings the Admiralty had decided that the Committee had served its purpose and it was time to return to the *status quo*.

Invincible, with Inflexible and Indomitable astern, at the Spithead Review of July 1909. (Author's collection)

Design and Construction 1905-14

ADMIRALTY WEEKLY ORDER No.351, 24 November 1911. All cruisers of the *Invincible* and later type are, for the future, to be described and classified as battlecruisers in order to distinguish them from armoured cruisers of the older type. (ADM182/2)

While the Committee on Designs was sitting it effectively took over the role of the Controller and the Board of Admiralty with regard to decisions on the designs being developed. Apart from this difference in consulting with higher authority, the DNC's department functioned normally in providing outline designs and suggestions, and then working out the chosen design in increasing detail. Following upon the Committee's First Progress Report, the Admiralty's design organisation returned to normal and the outline design resulting from the recommendation of Design 'E' by the Committee, was approved by the Board on 16 March 1905. This did not differ substantially from that recommended by the Committee except that the number of 12pdr guns was reduced from twenty to eighteen and there were some minor adjustment of the weights which, by 26 April, had increased the estimated displacement to 17,200 tons. The majority of this increase resulted from additions to the machinery and hull.[1] On 22 June 1905 the sheer, midship section, armour and rig drawings and legend of particulars were presented to and approved by the Board (see Table 9). Detailed calculations had resulted in a 10ft reduction in length, a 6in reduction in beam and a 50-ton increase in displacement, the latter again resulting from an increase in machinery weight, although in this case, entirely due to an additional 70 tons for oil fuel fittings. The detailed calculations for the new design were completed in August. (Detailed tables, for weights, dimensions, stability and construction can be found at the end of this chapter.)

The 1905-06 Programme provided for the construction of the *Dreadnought* and three of the new armoured cruisers. In June 1905 the latter had the provisional names *Invincible*, *Immortalite* and *Raleigh* but by the time they were laid down the last two names had been changed to *Indomitable* and *Inflexible*. Why there was only one battleship is not entirely clear but it seems likely that this was the result of her being chosen for rapid construction to prove the type and, in particular, to confirm that the turbine machinery and all-big-gun armament would be successful. In addition the available gun mounting and turbine machinery construction capacity made the accelerated con-

Table 9: *Invincible* class Legend of Particulars, 22 June 1905

DIMENSIONS:	567ft (oa), 530ft (pp) × 78ft 6in × 25ft (fore), 27ft (aft)
DISPLACEMENT:	17,250 tons load, 19,720 tons deep (excl oil)
MACHINERY:	41,000shp = 25kts
COAL:	1000 tons at load draught, 3000 tons max
OIL FUEL:	700 tons
COMPLEMENT:	708
ARMAMENT:	8 × 12in (80rpg); 18 × 12pdr (300rpg); 5 × 18in torpedo tubes (submerged)
ARMOUR:	Belt 6in amidships, 4in forward (extending 7ft 3in above and 4ft below LWL); bulkheads 7in and 6in; barbettes 7in; turrets 7in; CTs 10in and 6in; communication tubes 4in and 3in
PROTECTIVE PLATING:	Main deck 0.75in forward, 1in & 2in under 'A', 'P' and 'Q' barbettes and on crowns of lower CTs; lower deck 1.5in forward, 1.5in (flat) and 2in (slope) amidships, 2.5in aft; 2in splinter protection to base of barbettes; 2.5in torpedo protection bulkheads abreast magazines

WEIGHTS (tons):	
General equipment	660
Armament	2440
Machinery	3300
Engineer's stores	90
Coal	1000
Armour	3460
Hull	6200
BM	100
TOTAL:	17,250

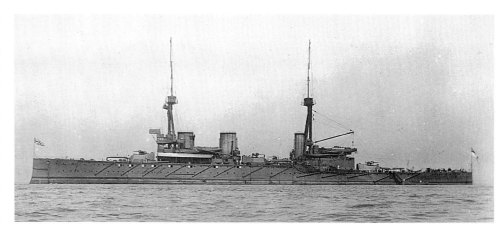

Indomitable as completed. (Author's collection)

struction of more than one vessel impossible and to the majority of the Board, if not Fisher, the battleship was the more important of the two types. *Dreadnought* was completed in January 1907 and, for a prototype, proved highly successful. She was followed by two further classes of similar design which increased the number of dreadnoughts in service to seven by mid-1910. The first of the *Invincible* class[2] ships was not laid down until February 1906, four months after *Dreadnought*, and the class did not complete until 1908. No further armoured cruisers of this type were to be laid down until 1909 although, as we shall see, this was not from any lack of interest on Fisher's part.

While under construction a number of changes were made to the *Invincible* design, the most important being a decision to fit *Invincible* with electrically-powered 12in mountings (see Armament chapter) which involved an additional weight of 130 tons, and the substitution of sixteen 4in guns for the original ATB armament of 12pdr guns. The alterations approved up to the time of completion are given in Table 10. These totalled 215 tons, an excess of 115 tons over the Board margin, while *Invincible* also had the additional 130 tons excess due to her electrically-powered gun mountings. However, none of the three ships greatly exceeded their designed displacement on completion and *Invincible*, allowing for her extra armament weight, actually came out slightly light. All three ships exceeded 26kts on their measured mile trials and, *as an interpretation of the design requirements*, they were very successful ships (with the sole exception of *Invincible*'s experimental 12in gun mountings!). For a few years they were also the most powerful cruisers in existence and to a great extent fulfilled Fisher's promise of being capable of sinking any ship fast enough to catch them and fast enough to escape from any ship that could sink them (given, of course, clear visibility, they would not have survived long in a close encounter with a *King Edward VII* or a *Lord Nelson*). However, with the completion of the first German battlecruiser in 1911 all this began to change.

The *Invincible* class were provided with various unofficial classifications to mark their difference from

Table 10: Approved modifications to *Invincible* class during construction

Sixteen 4in guns in place of 12pdr guns	65 tons
14in torpedoes and stores, and dropping gear for 50ft boats	5 tons
Fittings for keeping cable lockers clean	5 tons
Fittings for separate saluting magazine	2 tons
Substitution of cordite cases for air-tight lockers	40 tons
Armament office and domestics' mess	3 tons
Mastheads raised to 180ft above LWL	5 tons
Air-blast for 12in guns	5 tons
Magazine cooling machinery	30 tons
Increase in complement from 708 to 755	10 tons
Electric ring-main system	30 tons
Additional coal hoists	10 tons
Additions to bridge accommodation	5 tons
TOTAL:	215 tons

the older armoured cruiser type. These included cruiser-battleship, dreadnought cruiser and battlecruiser (the last used by Fisher himself at least as early as 1908) but it was not until late in 1911, with the issue of the Fleet Order quoted at the head of this chapter, that battlecruiser became their official designation.

Years of economy 1905-08

Although Fisher bowed to the opinion of his fellow officers that the *fully armoured* battleship remained the prime unit of a fleet he did so with obvious reluctance. Early in 1904 Fisher recorded that 'All are agreed that battleships must *for the present* be continued . . .', the emphasis on the 'for the present' being his and again, in the papers presented to Selborne in October 1904, 'At the present moment *naval experience is not sufficiently ripe to abolish totally the building of battleships* so long as other countries do not do so'. Fisher claimed on several occasions during his first term as First Sea Lord that while President of the Committee on Designs he wanted to build only the *Invincible*s and not the *Dreadnought* but was 'in a minority of one' (he also, in at least one letter, claimed that this view was supported by Lord Kelvin!). Late in 1905, shortly after *Dreadnought* was laid down and before any of the *Invincible* class had been started, he appears to have tried a different approach by proposing a 'fusing' of the two types. It is known that the DNC's department prepared outline designs for such ships in about November 1905 as the details of one, designated 'X4' and dated 2 December 1905 (see Table 11), are preserved in the Covers for the *Bellerophon* class battleships. Unfortunately the remainder (there were presumably at least an 'X1' to 'X3')[3] do not appear to have survived. The 'X4' design was essentially a 25kt version of *Dreadnought*, with the same armament and armour but with displacement increased from

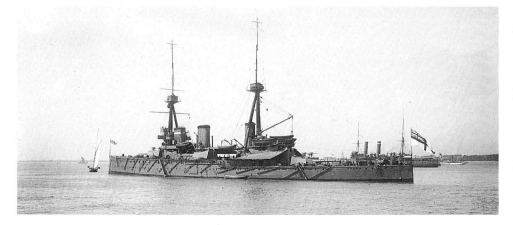

Inflexible at Spithead in July 1909. (Author's collection)

Table 11: Design 'X4', 2 December 1905

DIMENSIONS: 580ft (pp), 623ft (oa) × 83ft (max) × 27ft 6in (mean)
MACHINERY: 45,000shp = 25kts
ARMAMENT: 10 × 12in/45; 8 × 4in; 18 × 12pdr; 3 × 18in torpedo tubes
ARMOUR: Belt (amidships), barbettes, gunhouses and CT 11in

WEIGHTS (tons):

General equipment	750
Armament	3210
Machinery	3550
Coal	1000
Armour	6540
Hull	7350
Board Margin	100

LOAD DISPLACEMENT: 22,500 tons

17,900 tons to 22,500 tons to accommodate an expansion of the machinery power from 23,000shp to 45,000shp. This remarkable design, in anticipating the advent of the fast battleship by several years, would effectively have rendered the *Invincible* obsolete. Fisher seems to have missed the significance, judging by his continued advocacy of the big-gun armoured cruiser, presumably because he did not value heavy armour. Besides, with a little thought it is not difficult to see that any merging of the two types would result in a new type of battleship rather than an advanced form of armoured cruiser. In fact the whole idea tends to descend rapidly into a debate on semantics. In December or January the fusion proposal was considered by an Admiralty Committee which concluded that such a great increase in size and cost could not be justified and that the 1906-07 Programme should only provide for the construction of more ships of the dreadnought type and that for the present the three *Invincible*s fulfilled Britain's need for armoured cruisers.[4] This conclusion is understandable when it is considered that Britain was already constructing the most advanced armoured ships in existence. To move their development forward another stage at this early date must have seemed totally unnecessary. In any case the matter soon became academic as the replacement of the Conservative Government by a Liberal one following the Parliamentary elections of January 1906 quickly resulted in demands for further economy in naval spending. Consequently the Naval Estimates steadily declined over the next three years and there was little scope for any dramatic expansion of the construction programmes, either in numbers or in the power of individual ships. In the case of the armoured ships, the planned programme of four vessels per year was actually reduced to three in 1906-07 and 1907-08 and then two in 1908-09. In effect Fisher became the victim of his own success. The *Dreadnought* so paralysed foreign warship construction that there was for

some time no rival against which to maintain superiority, either in numbers or specification, and the British construction programmes were only required to maintain the existing design standard and build up a reasonable reserve. Fisher, subject to political pressure and attacks on his administration, soon began to justify Admiralty shipbuilding policy on the basis of how much further ahead Britain was in the construction of dreadnoughts (which number he tended to boost by the inclusion of the three *Invincible*s) than Germany, which by this time was regarded as Britain's only serious naval rival. In the case of the battlecruisers a more extended breathing space was obtained than with the battleships as details of the armament and speed of the *Invincible* class were initially kept secret. This led the Germans to the logical but incorrect conclusion that they would be standard armoured cruisers except for a uniform-calibre main armament. Therefore their initial answer was *Blücher*, a 15,590 ton armoured cruiser of 24.25kts armed with twelve 8.2in guns, laid down in February 1907. Germany's first true battlecruiser, the *Von Der Tann*, was not laid down until March 1908, the same year in which the three *Invincible*s were completed.

Despite the apparent lack of any major innovation in the development of the British 12in-gun dreadnoughts, more radical ideas *were* discussed in mid-1906 with regard to the armament to be employed in the 1907-08 Programme ships. These included twin and triple 12in gun mountings (for both 45- and 50-calibre guns) and 13.5in twin mountings. However, by December 1906 it had been decided to employ the same layout as that of the previous years battleship design and the only important change was in the adoption of the 12in/50cal gun. The 1907-08 programme provided for three of these vessels (the *St Vincent* class) and although no battlecruiser was included in the Programme plans were made, and approved, for such a ship.

The first of these appeared on 20 November 1906 when, it is assumed, they were submitted to the Controller, Rear-Admiral Jackson, by the DNC. Designated designs 'A', 'B' and 'C' (see Table 12), they were modified *Invincible*s with the wing turrets moved further apart, longitudinally, to increase their arc of training in cross-deck firing and to allow the use of both turrets simultaneously. In addition, in designs 'B' and 'C' only, the thickness of the belt armour for a length of 200ft on each side had been increased to 9in.[5] Design 'C' also had a 4in after belt, an innovation not present in the other two designs or *Invincible*. On the following day modified versions of 'A' and 'B' were produced ('C' having presumably been rejected) in which 12in/50cal guns were substituted for the 12in/45cal guns and the length, and in the case of 'B' the thickness of the armour belt, had been increased. On 22 November a third design, 'D', was produced,

Invincible entering Malta harbour in October 1913. By this date she was the only ship of her class which still had funnels of equal height – the fore funnels of *Inflexible* and *Indomitable* having been increased in height in 1911 and 1910 respectively in an attempt to reduce smoke interference to the bridge. The fore funnel of *Invincible* was eventually modified during her refit at Gibralter in Jan-Feb 1915. (R Ellis)

similar to 'B' but with further increases in the armour protection. All these designs were slightly slower than *Invincible* as they were larger but employed the same machinery (except 'D' where the increase in size necessitated a 43,000shp installation to keep the speed up to 24kts).

These designs were discussed at a Sea Lords' meeting on 22 November when the DNC was requested to produce a modified version of design 'D' with some adjustments to the distribution of armour and the 25kt speed of *Invincible* restored. This resulted in design 'E', of 5 December 1906, in which the main and upper belts were reduced in thickness by 1in and increased in length, protection was added aft and the torpedo protection bulkheads extended to cover the machinery spaces as well as the magazines (as had already been adopted in the *Bellerophon* class battleships of the 1906-07 Programme). This design was approved at a Board meeting on 11 December and on 19 December the DNC was authorised to begin the detailed design.[6] Although no battlecruiser was included in the 1907-08 Programme work on design 'E' continued for some time – presumably on the basis that it might be revived in the following year.[7]

Table 12: Battlecruiser designs for 1907-08 Programme

DESIGN:	A	B	C	A	B	D	E
DATE:	20/11/06	20/11/06	20/11/06	21/11/06	21/11/06	22/11/06	5/12/06
LENGTH (ft):	550	550	550	560	560	565	565
BEAM (ft):	79	79.5	80	81	81	81	83
DRAUGHT (ft):	26.25	26.5	26.75	26.75	27	27	27
SPEED (kts):	24.5	24.5	24.25	24*	24*	24	25
BELT (amidships):**	6in	9in/6in	9in/6in	9in/6in/4in	10in/6in/4in	10in/8in	9in
WEIGHTS (tons):							
General equipment	680	700	700	720	720	720	720
Armament	2600	2600	2600	2780	2780	2780	2780
Machinery	3420	3420	3420	3450	3450	3500	4100
Coal	1000	1000	1000	1000	1000	1000	1000
Armour	3600	3860	4180	4500	4650	5150	5200
Hull	6700	6820	6900	7150	7200	7450	7500
BM	100	100	100	100	100	100	100
TOTAL:	18,100	18,500	18,900	19,700	19,900	20,700	21,400

* On 22 November speed of 'A' was changed to 24.5kts and that of 'B' to 24.25kts.
** Armour and protective plating in 'A' of 20 November was as *Invincible*; in the other designs it was as *Invincible* except for the side armour. All designs carried an armament of 8 × 12in guns (45cal in those of 20 November and 50cal in rest), 16 × 4in guns and 5 × 18in torpedo tubes (later reduced to three in design 'E'). All designs had a maximum coal stowage of 3000tons. By June 1907 the following weights had been added to the estimate for design 'E': armament 180 tons, machinery 90 tons, armour 270 tons, hull 60 tons, increasing the load displacement to 22,000 tons.

In June 1907, political pressure for economy, reinforced by the apparently advanced state of Britain's dreadnought construction, prompted the Board to put forward a conservative building programme for the 1908-09 Estimates. This included one dreadnought and two armoured cruisers which, it was proposed, should revert to a 9.2in gun armament.[8] It is difficult to believe that Fisher would agree happily to this latter change, which would have meant abandoning his beloved battlecruisers, but it seems fairly certain that, at this time, his fellow Board members did not share his wholehearted belief in these ships. He was, however, still under pressure to reduce expenditure and a 9.2in gun ship would have been less costly (he was also somewhat preoccupied at this time by a dispute with Admiral Lord Charles Beresford, C-in-C Channel Fleet). Despite these efforts at economy the Cabinet rejected the Admiralty's Sketch Estimates in November and directed the First Lord, Lord Tweedmouth, to get them reduced. The programme was further modified to include, among other reductions, only one armoured cruiser but the Estimates were still rejected. This generated a major dispute between the Admiralty and the Government in which Fisher, who did not at this time see any major danger in a reduced programme and was concerned about accusations of Admiralty overspending, initially followed the government line. However, his hand was forced by the other Sea Lords, Vice-Admiral Sir W May and Rear-Admirals H Jackson and A Winsloe, who obtained Fisher's support, by threat of resignation, in a campaign to retain the 'modest' programme already proposed. In a memorandum to Tweedmouth dated 3 December, the four Sea Lords pointed out that, far from a reduction, an increase was required to counter the recently published construction plans of the German Navy and to avoid a major compensatory expansion of the 1909-10 Programme. Moreover, if, as suggested, the battleship was dropped from the Programme the effects would be serious not only to the maintenance of Britain's naval supremacy but on her gun and armour plate manufacturing plant (which relied on continuity of orders). The argument dragged on until February when, although the Cabinet did extract a further reduction in the Estimates, the modified Shipbuilding Programme, complete with its single battlecruiser (the 12in gun had by this time been reinstated), was accepted more or less intact.

The *Indefatigable* class

The new battlecruiser design followed the layout of design 'E' but omitted the improvements in side armour and underwater protection and reverted to the 45-calibre 12in gun. This was design 'A' (see Table 13) of 30 March 1908 which, judging by the designation may actually have been a reworking of the 'A' design of 20 November 1906. The design was essen-

Inflexible at Genoa on 5 March 1914. Since completion she has had her fore funnel raised in height, additional searchlight platforms added abreast the fore funnel and a new fore top fitted for her Argo rangefinder. Note that the torpedo net booms have been hoisted up parallel to the deck edge. (Author's collection)

tially an enlarged *Invincible* on which the only real improvement was the ability to fire the wing turrets across the deck without restriction and over a wider arc of fire (70°). If anything the design was weaker for, although she could claim a true, if restricted, broadside of eight guns and some small improvements in protection, the main belt abreast 'A' and 'Y' turrets was actually reduced in thickness to 4in. In the documents consulted there is no record of any preliminary discussions on this design or any variations for it, but it seems likely that the innovations of design 'E' were abandoned to reduce the size and save cost (the estimated displacement of design 'E' in June 1907 was 22,000 tons). It is also possible, of course, that Fisher objected to the ship being saddled with the extra armour. The final detailed design (see Table 13), with only minor changes from the March estimate, received Board approval in November 1908. It was decided that the new ship was to be named *Indefatigable* on 9 December 1908 and her construction began at Devonport Dockyard in February 1909.

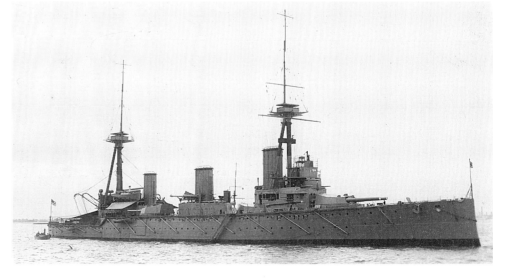

Indefatigable as completed. She was easily distinguished from her two half-sisters by the main top which was not provided in *Australia* and *New Zealand*. (Author's collection)

Indefatigable has been greatly criticised as showing no improvement on the *Invincible* class at a time when the Germans had begun the construction of a larger and better protected battlecruiser of her own – the *Von der Tann* (see Table 18) which was launched shortly after the *Indefatigable* commenced building. However, little information was available on the German ship at this time (the Germans having followed Fisher's lead and become very secretive). In the 1909 and 1910 editions of *Brassey's Naval Annual* the ship was credited with twelve 11in guns but even in the 1911 edition, where the armament is given correctly as eight 11in, the protection was still believed to be on a par with that of *Invincible*. The Admiralty did obtain more accurate information on the German ship somewhat sooner than this but not soon enough to allow any improvement to *Indefatigable*. Although she should not therefore be criticised on the basis of comparisons not available at the time, it should have been realised that the construction of battlecruisers by Germany effectively negated Fisher's principle arguments for such ships – which now faced the prospect of fighting an enemy on terms of, at the very least, equality rather than advantage.

The above excuse cannot, however, be offered in the case of *Indefatigable*'s two sister ships, *Australia* and *New Zealand*. These vessels were paid for by the Colonies after which they were named, in the case of the former to form part of the Royal Australian Navy and serve as its flagship, and in the case of the latter as an outright gift to the Royal Navy. These two ships were not laid down until June 1910 by which time British designs had moved on (see below) and the nature of German construction plans had become much clearer. A number of reasons might be advanced for the construction of these two ships, none of which can be supported by any direct evidence, but it seems likely that Fisher's influence was at work in giving preference to the battlecruiser type. For Australia the choice was more excusable in that the use of Second Class

Table 13: Design 'A' (*Indefatigable*) Legend of Particulars, November 1908

DIMENSIONS:	555ft (pp), 590ft (oa) × 80ft (max) × 26ft 6in (mean)
DISPLACEMENT:	18,750 tons (load)
MACHINERY:	43,000shp = 25kts
COAL:	1000 tons (load); 3000 tons (max)
OIL FUEL:	850 tons
COMPLEMENT:	737
ARMAMENT:	8 × 12in (80rpg); 16 × 4in (100rpg); 5 × Maxim MG; 2 × 18in submerged torpedo tubes
ARMOUR:	Belt 6in amidships, 4in at ends, 2.5in fore and aft (extending 7ft 6in above and 3ft 6in below LWL); bulkheads 3in and 4in forward, 4.5in and 4in aft; barbettes 7in; gunshields 10in and 7in; CT 10in (fore), 6in (aft); communication tubes 4in (fore), 3in (aft); signal tower 3in
PROTECTIVE PLATING:	Funnel uptakes 1.5in and 1in; torpedo bulkheads abreast magazines 2.5in; splinter protection to 12in gun hoists 2in; main deck 1in; Lower deck 1.5in (flat), 2in (slope) amidships, 2in fore and aft
WEIGHTS (tons):	
General equipment:	680
Armament:	2580*
Machinery:	3655
Coal:	1000
Armour:	3735
Hull:	7000
Board margin:	100
TOTAL:	18,750 tons

* Armament weight excludes shrapnel shells for 12in guns which was under consideration.

The original March 1908 legend differed from the above as follows: length (oa) 585ft, beam 80ft 6in, side armour extended to 7ft above and 4ft below LWL; weights (tons) – general equipment 665, armament 2540, machinery 3650, armour 3800, hull 6995.

Germany's first battlecruiser, *Von Der Tann*, seen here at the Spithead Coronation Review in 1911. (Courtesy R A Burt)

Table 14: Modified weights for *Australia* and *New Zealand*, 1909

	Indefatigable	*Australia*
GENERAL EQUIPMENT:	690	690
ARMAMENT:	2610	2615
MACHINERY:	3655	3655
COAL:	1000	1000
ARMOUR:	3735	3670
HULL:	7000	7070
BOARD MARGIN:	60	100
LOAD DISPLACEMENT:	18,750 tons	18,800 tons

battleships and large cruisers as flagships on distant stations was standard practice. This was certainly not the case with *New Zealand* and one can only conclude that in this case it was purely financial limits that controlled the choice of ship. There was of course, also the fact that Fisher's ability as a publicist had boosted the reputation of these ships in the public mind well beyond their true value.

The *Australia* and *New Zealand* were not exact copies of the *Indefatigable*, differing primarily in the arrangement of their armour forward and aft (see Armour chapter) There were also some minor alterations to the internal arrangements and the bridge structure, and the specified machinery power was increased from 43,000shp to 44,000shp although there was no corresponding increase in the required speed. These changes necessitated a slight alteration of the weights (see Table 14) which resulted in a 50-ton increase in the legend displacement (actually only 10 tons as the *Indefatigable* had by this time lost 40 tons from her Board margin).

The *Lion* class

On 8 September 1908 Fisher wrote the following, often quoted, passage in a letter to Lord Esher: '. . . I've got Sir Philip Watts into a new *Indomitable* that will make your mouth water when you see it! (and the Germans gnash their teeth).' It is unlikely, as is often assumed, that this refers to the *Indefatigable* as it was written several months after the outline design for that ship had been approved and only a short time before her design calculations were complete. A few days later, on 17 September, he wrote the following to the DNC:

My Dear Watts,
  Kindly send me a few lines to say whether any bright flashes of your genius have further illuminated our very fast big-gun battle cruiser *Indomitable*. We want to see her live! Let us call her 'Sanspareil'! But if we have to accept fewer guns, then let us call her the 'Incompatable.' For it will not be compatible with our brilliant progress if we do no more than just separate

the midship guns, which practically is all that a fewer-gun ship will give us in the shape of improvement.
  If we go to work the same way as we did with *Dreadnought*, we shall succeed, because [it is] so obviously silly to refuse an increase of 25 per cent of power in the 'Sanspareil', with only an increase of 4 per cent in cost and 5 per cent in displacement and to go into all the same docks (save one out of three at Malta) as the 'Incompatible' . . .[9]

Although to some extent this letter is incomprehensible without the background information that prompted it, it contains some clues as to what was under discussion at the time. It was at this time of year that early planning commenced for the following year's Naval Estimates, the proposed building programme, based on preliminary designs, normally being ready for Parliament in the spring. There was already concern about the extent of the German shipbuilding programme and suspicions that their ships would exceed those of the British in size, which meant they would have some advantage – as yet unclear, although they would at least be of closely-equivalent speed to British ships. Fisher must have realised that to maintain the advantages he claimed for the battlecruiser it would be necessary to increase speed still further. Judging by the 'very fast' statement, he had asked the DNC to look into designing such a ship and been told that this meant either a substantial increase in size or a reduction of armament weight. Fisher, in his usual fashion, seems to have been trying to minimise this problem which was, in any case, soon to evaporate.

Shortly after the argument over the 1908-09 Estimates was settled Tweedmouth was replaced by Reginald McKenna, a much more capable First Lord who did a great deal to advance the cause of the Navy in the Cabinet and in Parliament. At a meeting with the Sea Lords on 4 May 1908 he agreed that the 1909-10 Programme should include at least four armoured ships to compensate for the reduction in the previous year, and if necessary this might be increased to six. By the end of the year the Admiralty, having received intelligence of the expansion of Germany's shipbuilding and gun manufacturing capabilities, were convinced that Germany was accelerating her proposed construction programme and was about to mount a major challenge to Britain's naval supremacy. Consequently, on 8 December 1908, McKenna recommended the construction of six dreadnoughts to the Cabinet which precipitated another major conflict between the Cabinet and the Admiralty over the forthcoming estimates. Whatever the Cabinet's doubts concerning the reality of the Admiralty's contention, the argument soon spread to include the Opposition and the Press, and the Government quickly found itself under fire from all directions regarding its guardianship of the country's security. In February 1909, in the hope of quietening the furore, it was decided to put forward a Programme for four ships, as originally intended, but to provide for the possible German expansion by allowing for the construction of a further four 'contingent' vessels if this proved necessary. In announcing this decision in Parliament on 16 March, McKenna said that 'No matter what the cost the safety of the country must be assured' and went on to say that two of the ships would be laid down in July, two more in November and the remaining four later if required. This statement did not satisfy the Admiralty or the agitators as it was suspected that the last four ships might never be built or, if they were, those of the following year would be cut back. The Government eventually yielded to the continued pressure and in July announced that the four 'contingent' ships would definitely be laid down before the end of the 1909-10 Programme Year and would not prejudice the 1910-11 Construction Programme. Despite the impression given that the extra ships would be late additions, the British were in fact doing what they were accusing the Germans of doing – accelerating the Construction Programme. Battleships were normally laid down toward the end of the programme year (Dec-April) but the first two ships of the 1909-10 Programme (the battleships *Colossus* and *Hercules*) were laid down in July and the next two ships (the battleship *Orion* and the battlecruiser *Lion*) in November. The four contingent ships followed in April 1910 – towards the end of the normal time for construction to begin.

The new programme did not simply allow for an increase in numbers. The Admiralty were also greatly concerned about being outclassed on a qualitative level and gained approval for a substantial increase in the size and power of future battleships and battlecruisers. This was to be achieved by an increase in both gun power and, in the battlecruisers only, speed. The former took the form of the 13.5in gun, firing a 1250lbs projectile (compared with 850lbs for the 12in), approval for the design and manufacture of which had been given by Fisher on 21 October 1908 (one wonders if he picked Trafalgar Day deliberately!). This decision was too late for the first two ships of the Programme and Fisher was concerned that it might also be too late for the 'contingent' ships. On 5 March 1909 he wrote to McKenna: 'What so disquiets me now is that 4 of the German Dreadnoughts are of 22,000 tons and that cruiser 'H' will surpass the *Indomitable*. What an uproar there will be if we are over-classed. I ought to have pressed my convictions of a year ago to the bitter end for the more powerful 13½-inch gun armament. It is now too late, I fear, for the 4 ships to be laid down on April 1, 1910 [to be so armed]'.[10] It was not in fact too late for these, or the two earlier vessels laid down in November – the last six vessels, all armed with the 13.5in gun, became the four *Orion* class battleships and the two *Lion* class battlecruisers. That Fisher was still more interested in the battlecruiser type can be seen in another letter to McKenna written at the end of March 1909: 'We have to work hard in the next two years to build 8 'Nonpareils' to meet cruisers 'E', 'F', 'G' and 'H'. Cruiser 'E', the *Blücher*, has 8 11-inch guns and a speed of 25 knots – you want 28 knots to catch her!'[11] He was of course incorrect with regard to *Blücher* but was certainly justified in his concern about the other German ships which substantially outclassed their British opposite numbers. His demand for eight ships was not fulfilled, a pattern of one battlecruiser to each class of battleship being maintained for the next two Programme years, but he did get 28kts for the battlecruiser.

Before passing on to the *Lion* class design an occurrence during the discussions on the design of the *Orion* class is worthy of recording as illustrating Fisher's continued obsession with speed and his concern over the quality of German ships. On 12 May 1909, the Board of Admiralty, consisting of McKenna, Fisher, Jellicoe, Winsloe and the Civil Lord G Lambert MP (Bridgeman, the Second Sea Lord, was absent), met to discuss the proposed designs for the 13.5in-gun ships. The discussion on the battlecruiser was postponed for later consideration and effort was concentrated on the battleship designs which were for alternative 21kt and 23kt ships, the higher speed in the second design being obtained by an increase in size. The Board decided on the slower of the two, much to Fisher's disgust and he had his protest recorded in the Board Minutes in the following terms.

> In my judgement the alternative design for a battleship of 23 knots is preferable for tactical reasons to the 21 knot design adopted by the Board, in view of the evidence that the new German battleships are to have 30,000 Horse Power with a probable speed of 23 knots. It is not desirable we should be outclassed in any type of ship.
>
> The increased cost of £150,000, or £200,000, would be worth spending for the sake of equalling the alleged German speed.[12]

Discussion on the battlecruiser design was again postponed at Board Meetings on 17 and 26 May but on 27 May it was decided to adopt an eight-gun design with all turrets on the centre-line, two forward (with 'B' mounting superfiring over 'A'), one amidships and one aft. This decision simply followed the pattern set with the *Orion* class, the arrangement being identical except for the omission of the superfiring turret aft. Unfortunately the details of the designs which led up to this decision do not appear to have survived. The first design mentioned in the Ship's Covers is Design 'CV' (again one presumes there was a 'CI' to IV and possibly an 'A' and 'B') which was submitted by the DNC to the Controller, Jellicoe, on 7 June 1909 with the statement that it had been carefully revised and differed only slightly from that presented previously. Among the other comments that accompanied the rough drawings and legend (see Table 15) was that the DNC considered that 'For the purposes of comparison and in consequence of the increased armoured protection the new vessel may be regarded as a battleship as well as a cruiser.'[13] He also stated that if the ships length was increased by three frame spaces (12ft) an additional twin 13.5in mounting could be added aft to superfire over 'X' mounting. This was expected to add little to the cost of the ship but would add about £175,000 to the armament cost which, the DNC pointed out, was only a 7 per cent increase in overall cost for a 25 per cent gain in broadside fire. This idea was not taken up by the Board but it can be safely assumed that Fisher, at least, would have found this a very attractive proposal. The completed design for 'CV' was approved by the Board on 18 August 1909.

The improvement over the earlier British battlecruisers was dramatic, apart from the major increase in firepower the design provided for a 3kt increase in speed and a substantial increase in protection. The latter included a 9in belt and barbettes, while a 6in upper belt extended the side armour to the upper deck. However, the side armour abreast the forward and after 13.5in mountings was little better than that of *Indefatigable* and overall the design did not compare well with its German equivalents. This and other weaknesses in the protection meant that, despite the DNC's comment, they fell well short of the 'fast battleship' ideal. The cost of the high speed was marked, compared with the *Orion*, which had much heavier armour and carried ten 13.5in guns, the *Lion* was 7kts faster and 4000 tons heavier. From this time on British battlecruisers were consistently larger than their contemporary battleships.

Lion, like *Indefatigable*, was built by Devonport Dockyard, these two being the only battlecruisers built in a Royal Dockyard. Her sister ship, *Princess Royal* was put out to tender on 7 August 1909 and that from Vickers (dated 5 November) was accepted by telegram on 18 December.

In December 1909 the arrangement of armour was reconsidered, and resulted in a reworking of the protection at the forward and after end of the citadel (see Armour chapter). These changes involved a total additional weight of 210 tons. As 5.5 tons had already been appropriated from the Board Margin (3.5 tons for an increase in complement of 29, and 2 tons for an additional 30ft cutter), this left a surplus of 115.5 tons. On 24 January 1910 Jellicoe proposed that this be carried as additional weight and the fuel stowage be reduced to compensate. No reduction in fuel seems to have occurred and the completed ships were actually just light of their designed displacement.

Table 15: Design C5 (*Lion* class) Legend of Particulars, 7 June 1909

DIMENSIONS:	700ft (oa), 660ft (pp) × 88ft 6in × 28ft (mean)
DISPLACEMENT:	26,350 tons
MACHINERY:	70,000shp = 28kts
COAL:	1000 tons at load draught, 3800 tons max
OIL FUEL:	1000 tons
COMPLEMENT:	920
ARMAMENT:	8 × 13.5in (80rpg); 16 × 4in (150rpg); 5 × Maxim MG; 2 × 21in torpedo tubes (submerged)
ARMOUR:	Belt 9in (main), 6in (upper) amidships, 6in and 5in forward, 5in aft (extending 16ft above and 3ft 6in below LWL); bulkheads 5in forward, 9in and 5in aft; barbettes 9in and 8in; gunsheilds 10in and 7in; CT 10in; communication tube 4in
PROTECTIVE PLATING:	Upper deck 1in over citadel; lower deck 1in-1.25in amidships, 2.5in at ends; 1.5in and 1in funnel uptakes; 2.5in, 1.5in and 1in torpedo protection bulkheads abreast magazines
WEIGHTS (tons):	
General equipment	760
Armament	3260
Machinery	5840
Coal	1000
Armour	5930
Hull	9460
BM	100
TOTAL:	26,350 tons

The final approved legend of 18 August 1909 was as above except for the following:
Max coal stowage 3700 tons, oil fuel 1100 tons.
Complement 960.
Armour: after bulkheads 8in and 5in, barbettes 9in and 8in, gunshields 9in, communication tube 4in and 3in, Weights (tons) – general equipment 800, machinery 5340, armour 6140, hull 9710.

By early 1910 the armour had been further modified, the complement increased to 984 and the design weights adjusted as follows (tons) – general equipment 805, armament 3270, armour, 6400, hull 9660. The Board margin had been entirely absorbed and the design load displacement had increased to 26,475 tons.

All the ships of the 1909-10 Programme were designed with their fore funnels placed forward of the foremast. This layout, which had not been employed since the *Dreadnought*, was adopted because these ships, following decisions relating to fire control (see Armament chapter), had no main mast and it had therefore been decided to use the foremast as the main (heavy boat) derrick post – an arrangement that could only be employed if the mast was abaft the funnel.

Unfortunately, under certain conditions of wind direction and ships heading, the smoke and heat from the funnel could seriously interfere with the fore top and bridge to a much greater extent than was the case with the more normal arrangement. The heat was a particular problem as it could so raise the temperature of the mast that access to the foretop (which was via ladders inside the tripod struts) was totally cut-off.

These problems first revealed themselves in 1911 during the trials of *Hercules* and *Colossus* and, to a lesser extent, in *Orion* (her fore funnel served only six boilers whereas those of the two earlier ships served twelve). Although not ideal, it was decided that the existing arrangement in these ships could be accepted. The *Lion*, however, proved a very different case. Following her steam trials in January 1912 the Controller, Rear Admiral Charles Briggs, reported that he had seen the ship's Captain, A A M Duff, and:

> . . . it appears to be quite certain that the arrangements for control from the top and spotting from the spotting tower would be of little or no value for war. Presumably no ship would go into action without having fires in all boilers and in these conditions the fumes from the fore funnel would suffocate the operators in the top, who would also have a good chance of being burnt. It is not to be expected that the delicate instruments would be of any value there.
>
> The bridge is placed almost on top of the spotting

tower and consequently obscures the view with a slight roll. Rangefinders are placed in two turrets and guns could be controlled from them but I consider that neither of the turrets are suitable for the primary control. It therefore appears necessary to alter this state of things at once at the expense of delaying the completion of the ship and extra cost.

Proposals include to steer from the conning tower always and to fit a control tower abaft the conning tower, thus simulating the arrangement to those lately approved for the *King George V* class. The cost will probably not be less than £25,000 and time three months. As the ship is now in hand until middle of March for opening up machinery prior to acceptance, If this work is commenced at once the ship could be completed in early May. These remarks apply also to *Princess Royal*.[14]

In addition to these problems the upper bridge was 'uninhabitable' due to the heat and fumes, the manoeuvring compass was difficult to use and unreliable due to the proximity of the funnel and the signal flags and halyards were in danger of being burnt. In short her value as a fighting ship was seriously impaired. After some discussion it was concluded that the only solution was a complete rearrangement of the forward superstructure with the positions of mast and funnel reversed. The estimated cost was £25,000 per ship (the *Princess Royal* which was still fitting out had also to be

Lion as first completed with her foremast abaft the fore funnel. Note the low height of the second and third funnels, the unprotected 4in gun on the forward shelter deck, water measuring tank (for water consumption trials) abreast the main mast and the location of the conning tower under the bridge. (Author's collection)

altered) and it was hoped that the work would be completed in 3 months. In fact it cost over £30,000 per ship and the work took a few weeks longer. The main alterations were as follows:

(a) New fore funnel, 14ft in external diameter, fitted further aft.
(b) Heights of second and third funnel raised to same height as fore funnel (81ft above LWL).
(c) Existing main mast fitted in place of foremast, forward of new funnel.
(d) Positions of heavy and light boats reversed, former being repositioned abaft main mast and latter between first and second funnels.
(e) Foremast, without struts, refitted as main mast complete with boat derrick.
(f) Stump masts and derricks fitted abreast second funnel to serve light boats.
(g) New bridge structure constructed between CT and fore funnel. All structure within 20ft of compass built from naval brass.
(h) Conning tower enlarged and spotting tower removed.

Table 16: Legend of Particulars of *Queen Mary*, 1910

DIMENSIONS:	700ft (oa), 660ft (pp) × 89ft × 28ft (mean)
DISPLACEMENT:	27,000 tons
MACHINERY:	75,000shp = 28kts
COAL:	1000 tons at load draught, 3700 tons max
OIL FUEL:	1100 tons
COMPLEMENT:	999
ARMAMENT:	8 × 13.5in (80rpg); 16 × 4in (150rpg); 5 × Maxim MG; 2 × 21in torpedo tubes (submerged)
ARMOUR:	Belt 9in (main), 6in (upper) amidships, 6in, 5in and 4in forward, 5in and 4in aft (extending 16ft above and 3ft 6in below LWL); bulkheads 4in forward and aft; barbettes 9in and 8in; gunshields 9in; CT 10in forward, 2in aft; communication tube 4in and 3in forward; 4in battery 3in
PROTECTIVE PLATING:	Shelter deck 1in over 4in gun battery; forecastle deck 1.25in and 1in; upper deck 1in over citadel; lower deck – 1.25in amidships, 2.5in at ends; 1.5in and 1in funnel uptakes; 2.5in, 1.5in and 1in torpedo protection bulkheads abreast magazines

WEIGHTS (tons):	
General equipment	805
Armament	3300
Machinery	5460
Coal	1000
Armour	6575
Hull	9760
BM	100
TOTAL:	27,000 tons

Queen Mary

The battlecruiser of the 1910-11 Programme, although generally listed separately, was virtually a third unit of the *Lion* class with some minor improvements and changes. With her displacement increased to 27,000 tons it was necessary to increase the beam by 6in to restore the load draught to 28ft and, to maintain the speed of 28kts, the machinery power from 70,000shp to 75,000shp. In addition the forward 4in gun battery was provided with 3in armour protection and there were some minor changes to the distribution of the belt armour.

In December 1911, following the problems with *Colossus*, *Hercules* and *Orion* it was decided to reverse the positions of her forefunnel and foremast. The changes were along generally similar lines to those later adopted in *Lion* and *Princess Royal* except that the trunking for the fore funnel and the design of the bridge structure were slightly different and there were some minor changes to the distribution of the belt armour.

In February 1911, following a decision to adopt heavier projectiles for her 13.5in guns (see Armament chapter), 52 tons was appropriated from the Board margin for the extra load and in May 1911 a further 20 tons to provide for an after control tower with 6in armour walls. The remainder of the Board margin was absorbed in April 1912 when a third hydraulic pump was fitted for the main armament. As completed the ship was 230 tons light of her designed load displacement.

Tiger

The debate on the design of the 1911-12 Programme battlecruiser continued somewhat longer than in the case of earlier ships. As usual there appears to be no

Queen Mary in 1914. She could be distinguished from the *Lion* and *Princess Royal* by her wider second funnel, the absence of 4in guns on the forward shelter deck and the provision of a stern walk and the after torpedo/control tower. (Author's collection)

record of the early development of the design but in July 1911 Watts submitted three outline designs, 'A', 'A1' and 'C' (see Table 17) to the Controller for circulation to the Sea Lords, there is no mention of a design 'B' in the Ship's Covers and one must assume that this was rejected earlier. In the two 'A' designs the 13.5in mountings were disposed two forward and two aft, with 'B' and 'X' superfiring over 'A' and 'Y' turrets. In design 'C' the third turret was placed further forward, between the engine rooms and boiler rooms, which position, the DNC explained was found convenient because of the altered positions of bulkheads resulting from the introduction of an after torpedo room. This placed the turret abaft the masts and funnels and, unlike that in *Queen Mary*, gave it a clear arc of fire across the stern. The 'A' designs also had a 6in secondary gun battery, following upon a decision already arrived at for the battleships of the 1911-12 Programme (the *Iron Duke* class), with 5in armour protection which effectively increased the height of the side armour amidships by one deck. To accommodate the additional top weight the beam in the 'A' designs was increased to 91ft and to maintain the

required speed the specified engine power was also increased.

In discussing these designs the Sea Lords rapidly concluded that they preferred the 'A1' design generally but criticised the limited arcs of fire of the 6in guns on forward and after bearings and asked the DNC to look into improving this. In addition it was decided that in general layout design 'C' was preferable because 'two turrets so close together practically form one target, when sufficiently separated as in 'C' it means the enemy has three separate targets to fire at which complicates his fire control, this is important up to 10,000 yards'.[15] This resulted in the production of design 'A2', a variation on 'A1' with the armament layout of 'C', the embrasures of the forward 6in guns altered to allow them to fire 3° across the bow and the battery armour increased to 6in thickness. This (together with the three previous designs), was submitted to the Sea Lords on 14 August and received Board approval four days later. The DNC was asked to proceed with the design as rapidly as possible and this, apart from the usual minor changes, would probably have been an end to the matter but for a major political

Table 17: Battlecruiser designs for 1911-12 Programme

DESIGN:	A	A1	A2	C	A2	A2*	A2**
DATE:	July 1911	July 1911	July 1911	July 1911	12 Dec 1911	15 Dec 1911	15 Dec 1911
LENGTH (ft):	660	660	660	660	660	660	660
BEAM (ft):	91	91	91	89	90.5	90.5	90.5
DRAUGHT (ft):	28.5	28.25	28.25	28.25	28.25	28.33	28.5
DISPLACEMENT (tons):	28,450	28,100	28,100	27,250	28,200	28,300	28,500
SHP:	80,000	79,000	79,000	76,000	82,000	100,000	108,000
SPEED (kts):	28	28	28	28	28	29.5	30

ARMAMENT (all designs): 8 × 13.5in (80rpg)
Designs A and C 16 × 4in (150rpg), rest 16 × 6in (150rpg - increased to 200rpg in design A2 by November 1911)
Two 12pdr (design A only)
Five Maxim MG
Four submerged 21in torpedo tubes.

ARMOUR (all designs): Main belt 9in (amidships), 5in and 4in (fore and aft); upper belt 6in (amidships), 5in and 4in (fore), 5in (aft); lower belt 3in (not in design C); Side armour extending from 24ft 3in (24ft 6in in design C) above to 6ft (3ft 9in in design C) below LWL; bulkheads 4in (additional 2in bulkhead added forward in A2 design of December 1911); barbettes 9in and 8in; CT 10in (fore), 6in (aft); gunshields 9in: communication tubes 4in and 3in (for), 4in (aft); secondary gun battery 5in (4in in design C; increased to 6in in A2 design of December 1911).
PROTECTIVE PLATING: Shelter deck 1in over 6in gun battery in design A2 only, 1in over 12pdr guns in design A only; forecastle deck 1.5in (1in and 1.5in in design A and in design A2 of December 1911); upper deck 1in over citadel except under secondary gun battery; main deck 1in outside citadel; lower deck 1in amidships, 3in (2.5in in design C) forward; torpedo bulkheads 2.5in, 1.5in and 1in; funnel uptakes 1.5in and 1in.

WEIGHTS (tons):

General equipment	820	820	820	820	840	840	840
Armament	3860	3650	3650	3450	3650	3650	3650
Machinery	5780	5720	5720	5500	5550	5650	5900
Fuel	1000	1000	1000	1000	1000	1000	900
Armour	7030	6980	6980	6730	7360	7360	7360
Hull	9860	9830	9830	9650	9650	9650	9770
BM	100	100	100	100	100	100	100
TOTAL:	28,450	28,100	28,100	27,250	28,200	28,300	28,500

change in the Board of Admiralty as a result of demands for the formation of a Naval War Staff.

In October 1911 the Home Secretary, Winston Churchill, exchanged posts with Reginald McKenna and shortly afterwards the Board was reconstituted in line with the new First Lord's wishes. Of the original Sea Lords only the Controller, Rear-Admiral Briggs, was to remain. Admiral Sir A K Wilson (the First Sea Lord since Fisher's departure) was replaced by Admiral Sir Francis Bridgeman, Vice-Admiral Sir G Le C Egerton (the Second Sea Lord) was replaced by Vice-Admiral Prince Louis of Battenberg and Captain C E Madden (the Fourth Sea Lord) by Captain W Pakenham. One of Churchill's first moves was to seek the advice of Fisher who, during three days of discussion at Reigate Priory, was 'most of all . . . stimulating in all matters related to the design of ships'.[16] Churchill was soon infected with Fisher's great obsessions for speed, gun power and all oil-fired boilers, and carried these back to the Admiralty where the new Board took up its duties on 5 December 1911.

Churchill was much more inclined to become involved in the details of warship design than was normal for a First Lord and on 20 November 1911 requested that the tender for the armoured cruiser be delayed while he made a few inquires into the design. This inquiry appears to have resulted in a proposal to increase the speed of the new ship. On 12 December 1911 the final design of 'A2' was approved by the Board 'subject to certain modifications to secure additional horse power.' On the same day Churchill asked if the boilers of all the armoured ships of the 1911-12 Programme could be adapted to use oil fuel only.

On 15 December Watts submitted to the Controller modified legends designated 'A2*' and 'A2**'. In 'A2*' the machinery power was increased to 100,000shp for a speed of 29.5kts at the cost of an additional 100 tons displacement and an increased sinkage of 1in. In 'A2**' the power was further increased to 108,000shp for a speed of 30kts, which added 300 tons to the displacement and 3in to the draught, and her fuel was modified to half coal/half oil. It was also necessary in 'A2**' to increase the width of the boilers and boiler rooms. Watts added that the machinery could be modified to oil-fuel only but that 'to carry the same amount of fuel oil would require some to be carried above the protective deck which is undesirable and the loss of protection by giving up coal above this deck would be considerable.'[17]

Rear-Admiral Briggs appears to have passed on the details of 'A2**' only, with the comment that all oil-fuel arrangements could be adopted at little added cost provided the decision was not delayed. However, he was more inclined to favour the increased oil stowage in combination with coal, as recommended by the DNC, as the additional oil would assist in attaining the speed and valuable experience would be gained in the design and construction of the oil stowage arrangements. On 20 December, the day after design 'A2**' received approval, the DNC suggested that the inner bottom compartments could be employed for additional oil-fuel stowage and if all these were fitted with the necessary pipes, valves etc, the maximum fuel stowage could be increased to 7350 tons (3750 tons oil/3600 tons coal) in an emergency. This proposal was approved by Briggs on the following day. Detailed design resulted in a reduction of these figures to 6800 tons (3480 tons oil/3320 tons coal) in the completed ship, however, under normal circumstances the maximum stowage was not expected to exceed 2450 tons oil and 2450 tons coal and during the First World War the normal maximum actually carried was 800 tons oil and 3240 tons coal.

On 2 March 1912 a tender from J Brown (dated 23 January) was provisionally accepted for the new ship which was to become HMS *Tiger*. A final letter of acceptance was sent on 3 April 1912 and the contract was signed on the following day.

The main alterations made to the ship between the approval of the design and completion were:

(a) On 10 February 1912 it was approved to fit anti-rolling tanks and these were incorporated in the design. In June 1912 it was decided that these should not be fitted and the bilge keels were increased in depth from 18in to 2ft 6in instead.

(b) On 27 February 1912 the funnel heights were raised 5ft to 81ft above the LWL, in line with alterations already incorporated in the *Queen Mary* and the *Lion* class.

(c) On 27 July 1912 it was approved to fit additional oil-fuel sprayers to the boilers. The additional weight of 27.5 tons was appropriated from the Board margin.

(d) In 1913 it was approved to fit the ship with two 3in AA guns.

(e) The number of 3pdr saluting guns was reduced from six to four.

(f) In 1913 it was approved to omit the torpedo net defence, saving 95 tons.

On completion the ship was 70 tons light of her designed load displacement.

The *Tiger* was the last, and easily the best, of the pre-war British battlecruisers. Her deeper side armour (courtesy of the 6in gun battery), heavier secondary armament, higher speed and improved arcs of fire making her a major step forward in the design evolution of the British battlecruiser. She was nevertheless, like the *Queen Mary*, a derivative of the *Lion* design and still retained some of the weaknesses of that ship – in particular a reduction in the side armour abreast the forward and after barbettes.

The 1912-13 Programme included the five *Queen Elizabeth* class battleships which marked a major

Tiger in 1916-17. Note the searchlight mounted on the roof of 'Q' turret. (Imperial War Museum: SP1674)

advance in the evolution of the type in that they revived the idea of a true 'fast battleship' of the type envisaged during 1905-06. They were designed for the same speed as the *Invincible* class – 25kts – but were 10,000 tons larger and armed with 15in guns. They also had heavier protection than any of the earlier British dreadnoughts and represented a true 'fast wing' squadron that was more than capable of standing in the line against opposing battleships. They were by no means perfect but were, for their time, a major advance in armoured ship technology which should have brought the development of the battlecruiser to an end. This they did for a while but shortly after the outbreak of the First World War Fisher returned to the Admiralty with his faith in the original battlecruiser concept undimmed.

Table 18: German battlecruiser designs 1907-13

Ships	Laid down	Completed	Load displacement (tonnes)	Armament	Belt armour (in)	Barbettes armour (in)	shp	Speed (kts)
Blücher	1907	1911	15,600	12 × 8.2in 8 × 5.9in 4 × 17.7in TT	7	7	34,000(ihp)	24.25
Von Der Tann	1908	1911	19,000	8 × 11in 10 × 5.9in 4 × 17.7in TT	10	9	43,600	24.75 (27)
Moltke Goeben	1908 1909	1912 1912 }	22,600	10 × 11in 12 × 5.9in 4 × 19.7in TT	11	9	52,000	25.5 (28)
Seydlitz	1911	1913	24,600	10 × 11in 12 × 5.9in 4 × 19.7in TT	12	9	63,000	25.5 (28)
Derfflinger Lützow	1912 1912	1914 1916 }	26,200	8 × 12in 12 × 5.9in 4 × 19.7in TT	12	10	63,000	26.5 (28)
Hindenburg	1913	1917	26,500	8 × 12in 14 × 5.9in 4 × 23.6in TT	12	10	72,000	27.5 (28.5)

Notes: The armoured cruiser *Blücher* is included for comparison. 8.2in gun = 21cm; 11in gun = 28cm; 12in gun = 30.5cm; 5.9in gun = 15cm; 17.7in TT (torpedo tube) = 45cm; 19.7in TT = 50cm; 23.6in TT = 60cm. The gunshield armour was generally equal to the barbette armour. The main belt armour extended over the full length of the machinery and magazine spaces. The figures in parentheses under speed are the maximum service speeds at full power with clean hull, clean boilers and reasonable sea conditions (the horsepower given is the nominal design figure which was always greatly exceeded on trial).

The German battlecruiser *Moltke*, interned at Scapa Flow, 1919. (Author's collection)

Table 19: Battlecruiser construction 1906-14

Name	Builder	Machinery	Laid down	Launched	Commissioned
Invincible	Armstrong Whitworth	Humphrys, Tennant	2 Apr 1906	13 Apr 1907	20 Mar 1909
Inflexible	J Brown	J Brown	5 Feb 1906	26 Jun 1907	20 Oct 1908
Indomitable	Fairfield	Fairfield	1 Mar 1906	16 Mar 1907	20 Jun 1908
Indefatigable	Devonport Dky	J Brown	23 Feb 1909	28 Oct 1909	24 Feb 1911
Lion	Devonport Dky	Vickers	29 Nov 1909	6 Aug 1910	4 Jun 1912
Princess Royal	Vickers	Vickers	2 May 1910	29 Apr 1911	14 Nov 1912
New Zealand	Fairfield	Fairfield	20 Jun 1910	1 Jul 1911	19 Nov 1912
Australia	J Brown	J Brown	23 Jun 1910	25 Oct 1911	21 Jun 1913
Queen Mary	Palmers	J Brown	6 Mar 1911	20 Mar 1912	4 Sep 1913
Tiger	J Brown	J Brown	6 Jun 1912	15 Dec 1913	3 Oct 1914

Table 20: Summary of design calculations for battlecruisers 1905-12

CLASS:	Invincible	Indefatigable	Lion	Queen Mary	Tiger
DATE*:	10 Aug 1905	cDec 1908	25 Sep 1909	cAug 1910	cJan 1912
COEF OF FINENESS:	0.558	0.558	0.564	0.575	0.554
LOAD CONDITION (tons):					
General equipment	660	680	800	805	845
Armament	2440	2580	3260	3295	3660
Machinery	3300	3555	5190	5310	5630
Engineer's stores	90	100	150	150	125
Coal	1000	1000	1000	1000	450 coal/450 oil
Armour and protective plating	3460	3735	6140	6575	7400
Hull	6200	7000	9710	9765	9580
Water in anti-rolling tanks (Tiger only)					250
Board margin	100	100	100	100	100
LOAD DISPLACEMENT:	17,250	18,750	26,350	27,000	28,490
DEEP CONDITION (tons):					
General equipment	740	872	1038	994	980
Armament	2480*	2628*	3346*	3390*	3660
Machinery	3300	3591	5190	5310	5630
Engineer's stores**	90	100	150	150	125
Coal	3000	3100	3700	3700	2450
Armour and protective plating	3460	3735	6140	6575	7400
Hull	6200	7000	9710	9765	9580
Reserve feed water	350	427	590	590	620
Overflow feed water	n/a	27 (half full)	140 (full)		80
Oil fuel	700	850	1130	1130	2450
Water in anti-rolling tanks (Tiger only)					395
Board margin	100	100	100	100	100
DEEP DISPLACEMENT:	20,420	22,430	31,234	31,844	33,470
LIGHT CONDITION – items to be removed from legend condition (tons):					
Coal	1000	1000	1000	1000	450
Oil	n/a	n/a	n/a	n/a	450
Fresh water	70	70	84	84	90
Provisions	40	40	48	49	50
Officers stores and slops	45	45	45	45	50
Half WO's stores	33	37	45	47	47
Half Engineer's stores	45	50	75	75	63
Water in anti-rolling tanks (Tiger only)					250
TOTAL:	1233	1242	1297	1300	1450
LIGHT DISPLACEMENT:	16,020	17,508	25,053	25,700	27,040